Take A Deep Breath...

It's

Christmas

---

*A 40 Day Journey
Towards The Heart Of Christmas*

---

by K.L. Kandel

*Linda
EX 14:14
PS 46:10*

*Karen
Luke 2:10 & 11*

*Kathie
John 1:14*

*Kris
Phil. 1:12*

ISBN-13: 978-0615892696

Unless otherwise identified, all Scripture quotations
in this publication are taken from the Holy Bible:
New International Version. (2011). Grand Rapids,
Mich.: Zondervan. Used by permission; and the
King James Version (KJV).

Dedication

We met our mother a number of years ago. Aside from the doctors and nurses in the delivery room, hers was the first and sweetest face we looked into as we entered this life. With every birth she waited to hear that first breath followed by a cry.

During the writing of this book, ours were the last faces that she looked into as she took her final breath and entered her new life. Suddenly our mother saw the sweetest and most glorious face of all, her Lord and Savior, Jesus.

This book is dedicated to our mother, Nadine Kandel. In those final moments she opened her eyes very wide and with one last breath she saw the reality of the gift of Christmas and one of the last things she heard us say was, "Take a deep breath, Mother, it's Heaven!"

Table Of Contents

*Includes recipe

Intro

Christmas is an incredibly busy time of year, so we wanted a short book that would be a quick read, an appetizer, a petite bouche, a little bite of something savory or sweet, but something that promises more to come. This book is not designed to fill you up. This book is designed to make you hungry. Please know that we never want anything we write to replace your own time of reading the Scripture, studying, praying, spending time with the Lord. That is an extremely important time, because God speaks. Sometimes He whispers, sometimes He shouts, but God does speak to us through His Word.

The petite bouche in the culinary world means a small bite and is designed by its nature to wake up the taste buds for what else is to come, the main course, the meat and potatoes, the salad greens and of course the sweetest of desserts. So here is a little something, a tiny bite of the sweetness of Christmas.

But to go along with this little bite, we need a sip of something. Our choice...coffee.

There are tea drinkers, and we suppose they really like tea, but then there are those of us who drink coffee. For us, it's not a matter of like, but love.

Coffee drinking is, in reality, a love affair. There is that first smell of its bitter brew in the AM, that first sip when your eyes are barely open as its soothing warmth beckons you to wake up. Even the rich caramel or even taupe color is compelling. We like ours with a little, or a lot, of cream. Yep! Coffee drinking is about love and for us it's about Christmas.

We have loved coffee from the first taste as children. It was not a learned habit, oh no, rather an instant delight. Our parents thought we were too young to drink it on a regular basis, so it was a special rare treat reserved for Christmas morning. Christmas toast and sweet maple flavored rolls were especially delicious dunked in our Christmas coffee. Coffee...Christmas...as far as we're concerned the two go hand in hand.

So grab a cup of your favorite blend or your tea, if you must, and let's explore the wonder of the Christmas season. Let's taste the sweetness and forget about the crowds, the busyness, the hub-bub, the shopping nightmares and just savor every drop of Christmas. Take a deep breath, relax, smell the pine, the freshness, the spices, the smell of the scotch tape and indeed the coffee. Yes, breathe it all in, it's Christmas.

Let us introduce ourselves to you. We are Kris Kandel Schwambach, Karen Kandel Kizlin, Kathie Kandel Poe and Linda Kandel Mason, four sisters with some very different life experiences. We would like to walk through the Christmas season with you because we love Christmas.

Christmas is a time to laugh, maybe wipe away a tear, to sing, to worship. So for these moments over the holidays, would you give us the privilege of opening our lives to share a few stories and opening the Scripture to see the majesty and mystery of THE GIFT behind each gift?

Day 1

Expectation...it's the light in the eyes of a child at Christmas. It's the wonder on the face of a soon to be mother. It's the hope in the step of the young man carrying the ring. It's the look of anticipation as someone opens the perfect gift at Christmas.

The gift was given. There it sat on my lap. The giver has always exhibited the most excellent taste and always has known the exact thing to buy. So there it was. This was going to be fun. Beautifully wrapped, meticulously tied with a gorgeous bow, I carefully salvaged the paper on this most anticipated present. What could it be? An artful piece of pottery? No, it wasn't quite heavy enough. A purse? She knows me, ahh yes, a purse because she knows me well. Yes indeed...but then, there it was. I reached into the recesses of my brain to pull out its name. Finally the nerve endings made the jump over the synapse and the name came to me as I lifted it out of the box. I was in a quandary. How could I make my face appear joyous, thrilled, delighted? This was lederhosen...LEDERHOSEN? LE-DER-HOSEN! You know lederhosen, you've seen it. It's Oktoberfest garb, shorts with bibbed suspenders, mostly worn by men carrying German steins.

Later, I carried it back to the bedroom, my husband by my side. As I walked I reflected. I kept asking myself, "What about me screams lederhosen? Why had I not been more specific on my Christmas list? Why had I not said 'NO LEDERHOSEN'? Had I said I wanted something embroidered?"

Back in the privacy of our room I looked at my husband and said, "As wunderbar as this is, ummm, I'm not sure I can wear it." He looked at me with his big sympathetic eyes that said it all, "She forgot a book on yodeling and a long alpine horn."

Expectation...and how does the old poem go? Mama in her kerchief and I in my...lederhosen? Yes, it's the lederhosen syndrome. And this is often how the Christmas season feels. We build up the moments. We expect high fashion, designer, haute couture and sometimes what we get is lederhosen. But can you see the gift behind this gift? Leder-hosen may not have been a gift I could wear but it has been a gift I have thoroughly enjoyed. Over the years, I have smiled, laughed at the look on my husband's face, retold the story. A purse would have long since been retired. Laughter burns calories, raises tests scores, wards off diseases and helps with pain tolerance. And that is a gift! By the way there are web sites where you can order your own lederhosen...they promise fast delivery.

Luke 1

Expectation...can you feel it? Do you sense it? Let's experience the Bible, for we are about to open the most magnificent book ever written. We're about to walk into the presence of the King. We're about to fellowship with the One who knows us by name. Sense the awe, the majesty, the wonder. Pray, "Lord, please open my mind so I can understand Your Word."

And so we begin:
Luke 1:1-4 says that many had undertaken to draw up an orderly account of the Messiah, and yet, God called Luke to do it too. Luke was an unlikely candidate. He wasn't one of the twelve. Was he Jewish? He was most likely a Gentile. The Bible doesn't say for sure. We know he was a doctor, but what did that mean? Some physicians at that time were slaves. God called him to write down the Scripture, but how many doctors do you know that you can even READ their handwriting. No, Luke might not have been the likely choice but He was God's choice. That tells me that even if many others are called to do something, even if I don't feel like I'm a likely candidate, there is still room for me. God can still use me. So I wonder, during this Christmas season what God wants to do in me, through me, with me, and for me, and for you as well. An adventure awaits.

Day 2

What kicks off the Christmas Season for you? Is it that first Christmas commercial aired in October? Is it the holiday music piped into the stores? Is it Christmas catalogues arriving in the mail? Regardless of what launches you into that holiday feeling, we are beginning with Thanksgiving. I want you to understand, I am not talking about just the day, I am talking about the heart. Let me share a few moments of thanksgiving.

Crisp cold air on a June morning, the steam from my coffee rising as I set foot onto the balcony of a condo, the snowcapped Grand Teton Mountains in the distance, moose munching their breakfast just moments away, herds of buffalo, elk and wolf packs, I can't take it all in. The majesty is too much to hold in my mind, but my heart overflows with gratitude to a God who cared so much He would provide such exquisite scenes. This is thanksgiving.

Waves slap the beach. The giant ocean stretches out before me. So many flowers, and colors, and kinds, they can't be counted. Whales seem to rise out of the air with little effort considering their enormous size. Exotic birds sing out their songs and display their glorious colors. My heart sings its song of joy over beauty that words aren't big enough to express.

Thanksgiving seizes my soul. Tears flood my eyes.

The steam rises off of the distant mountains so that they appear smoke covered. These mountains aren't quite as big, they have a different personality from their western cousins, but they are equally as stunning. Big black bears lumber across the winding road, a mama and her triplet cubs, a rare treat. Trees heavy with green gorgeous leaves hide other wildlife, some I've never laid eyes on. Wild pigs are known in this area of the Great Smoky Mountains. I've just never seen them. I want to sing or dance or somehow record the beauty, but words fail. I can only tell God, with my limited vocabulary, how grateful I am. It's good He can see into my heart. He can witness the overflow of thanksgiving.

I look. Beautiful black eyes, just minutes old, stare into mine. Awe, wonder, amazement, joy unspeakable, thanksgiving, she doesn't yet know that I'm her grandmother. She doesn't yet know that her little life has just changed mine forever. I will never have enough words, or big enough words, or fancy enough words, to tell God thank You for my children and grandchildren. Their first laugh, one of the sweetest sounds this side of heaven, has always been answered with my laughter. Their cries make my heart cry. How could I possibly express this gratitude that I feel? I try, but fail.

Pumpkin pie cools on the counter. Its spicy sweetness beckons me to taste. The turkey roasts, sending out its tasty aroma, an invitation to indulge. Cranberries are on the table, but the brilliant red color is in the trees as well. Pumpkin orange, golden yellow, olive green and rusty brown leaves float by my window in showers. Soon the house will be filled with an abundance of food and an abundance of people. Thanksgiving! We set aside a day each year to be grateful, to express our thankfulness to our Creator. Why? Because we were made for it. We were created to enjoy beauty, splendor, exquisite sights, sounds, smells, tastes of creation and respond with gratitude.

Sometimes we think about Heaven and anticipate sitting on a cloud, bored out of our minds, playing a little harp. NOT SO! All the beauty that we see here, all the gorgeous scenes that so fill our hearts and soothe our souls are nothing compared to the exquisite beauty that awaits us in Heaven. Thanksgiving won't be just a day, or a brief moment, but the place where we live. Our grateful hearts will burst with song and joy and rest and healing and beauty, and well, you get the picture. The very thing that we get snatches of here, the very thing that blows our minds and sings in our souls here, will be the state in which we live there. Thanksgiving Day is a beginning. Enjoy it well today. It is the prelude to all the Thanksgivings to come.

**Linda's perfect pumpkin pie recipe
for your Thanksgiving**

First you get those pants that fishermen wear because pumpkin patches can be muddy. With your outfit on, proudly look for the best pumpkin in the patch. Okay, you may have to walk seven miles because you are making the best pumpkin pie ever. When you get your pumpkin, look it over carefully for any bad places. If you are satisfied with your choice head for home.

At home wash the pumpkin thoroughly. Cut the pumpkin in half. Pumpkins are hard to cut so don't cut off your fingers. Discard that nasty, stringy stuff called pulp from the inside of the pumpkin. Remove the stem and discard. You can save the seeds to dry and roast but I wouldn't because they are disgusting.

Preheat the oven to 190 degrees centigrade. I am not telling the fahrenheit cause you need to figure that out for yourself. Well, okay...350 degrees.

Place pumpkin halves face down in a shallow baking dish until tender. This could take all day so be patient because patience is a fruit of the spirit.

Once the pumpkin has cooled, scoop out the flesh, puree and mash it. If you want this silky smooth, you can run it through a sieve.

Oh yeah, take off those fisherman pants.

Or you could buy a can of pumpkin.

1 large can of pumpkin (or 29 ounces of freshly
pureed pumpkin)
1 cup white sugar
1 cup brown sugar
1 tablespoon heaping full of flour
5 teaspoons of pumpkin pie spice
A pinch of ginger
2 teaspoons of salt
1/2 teaspoon of vanilla
6 eggs
1 quart (4 cups) milk
1 cup evaporated milk

Mix and pour into three unbaked pie shells

Bake 450 degrees 15 minutes, reduce heat to 350
degrees for 45 minutes or until a knife inserted into
the center comes out clean.

Luke 1

Luke 1:1-4 tells us that Luke has carefully investigated everything from the beginning. Remember, Luke is a physician. I have doctors in my family. They are methodical, thorough, exacting and careful to get details just right. The Scripture also tells us that he writes an orderly account. I like order.

However things can get a little "un-orderly" at this time of year. Or maybe it goes beyond disorder and feels much more like chaos. Or maybe even the circumstances in your life are so overwhelming that you feel like you are in a free fall. Cancer, surgeries, divorce, death, all of these are over the cliff events.

But disorder, chaos and even devastation do not have to be defining for us. Giving thanks is not about the circumstances but rather about victory through them. It is about thanking God and knowing that He is there. What He carries us into, He will carry us through.

So today, let's spend a few moments in the orderly account and renew our spirits. Go back and read Luke 1:1-4, the account in Luke is thoroughly investigated, trustworthy, and orderly.

He is writing so we can know the CERTAINTY of the Word. He will show us how the birth and life of Jesus fulfilled Scripture. We are going to see miracles, long promised, fulfilled. That treasure fills me with great gratitude and thanksgiving.

Day 3

Never did I want to shop on Black Friday, too many people, too many cars, too much chaos. It was the day to drive to our favorite tree farm, pick out the most beautiful, seven foot, perfectly formed Christmas tree, cut it down, drag it home, set it up, make sure it didn't fall over, (we weren't always successful at that; my sister's husband nailed theirs to the floor), decorate it, and, whew, set the Christmas holidays in motion. Yep, that's how it was supposed to be done.

And then, as our children pointed out, we moved to the dark side. A January, 90% off sale of a perfect, seven foot, dark green, never to topple, artificial Christmas tree convinced me to succumb. This tree could be set up in October, if I so chose, with nary a fallen needle. I could decorate at my leisure and not have to schedule the tree cutting around the Nebraska/Oklahoma football game my husband had to watch or the team would know and refuse to win.

My plan for the day after Thanksgiving was a free day...sleeping in, rest, feet up, good book (The TV had the game on, remember), because the Christmas tree was already bought, up, decorated, sparkling beautifully away in the window. Left-overs were in the fridge. Turkey, dressing, mashed potatoes, a few moments in the micro-wave and dinner would be ready. Ah, the wonder of the modern world. I went to bed on Thanksgiving night with visions of leisure dancing around in my head.

And then... the 3:00 AM hot flash. Hot flashes on a cold November morning don't warm your heart, they wake you up. Sweating, dripping, wanting to run outside and roll in the cold, crispy snow or open the freezer and crawl in. Hot flashes are intense, stinging surges of painful heat. I seriously don't get why someone hasn't properly harnessed this un-tapped resource. It could resolve the energy crisis.

So on this, my sleeping-in day, I was up at 3:00 AM, Bible in one hand, coffee in the other. But frankly I love these quiet moments with my Best Friend. He never sleeps and always meets me in these quiet times.

By 5:00 AM an idea came, "Why not go out for a little shopping." I ran upstairs, quickly dressed, and gently whispered to my husband that I was going out to shop. He grunted. Fortunately, I speak hus-band and understood perfectly what he meant. "Go, have fun! I love you and spend a lot of money." OK, I don't always get the translation quite right.

I was off in the darkness of the November morning. Not a car was on the street. How bad would this be? No one else was even up. Suddenly, another thought, "I'll bet my sister is up too. We're cut out of the same cloth. She probably had the same hot flash." Her house was on the way. I'd just drive by and see if her light was on. Sure enough, there she was, Bible in hand, coffee in the other. I'm telling you, they just go together. She saw my car stop, but couldn't make out who it was. I scared her half to death when I knocked at that early hour. "It's me. Do you want to go shopping? I'm going to Walmart."

Need I ask? She ran upstairs to check with her husband. He grunted out the same blessing. Love these guys. Again, by her house there was hardly a car. Seriously, how bad would this be? NO one was up. We would get to Walmart, run in, run out, be back before anyone really knew we were gone.

Surprise! The parking lot was jammed. We parked a million miles away (maybe we could burn off a few of those Thanksgiving calories) and ran for the doors just as they were opening. The crowd was enormous, the check-out line even bigger. But we had become grandmothers over the last year and those little ones were worth the death defying battle. We found treasure, too many deals, stood way too long in line, but finally we were back outside. We got to the car. We came. We saw. We survived. We had conquered Walmart. It was time to take our prizes home. There we were, smugly heading home, and then we saw it. TARGET! We were in deep!

Luke 1

I love to study the Scripture. There is always something new. It is a hunt for treasure. Today, in Luke 1:1-10, Zechariah is chosen to serve in the Temple, an auspicious day to say the least. Since there were so many priests, this happened at best only once in a lifetime. Was he nervous, excited, or overwhelmed?

What strikes me here is that all the assembled worshipers were outside praying. Did you catch that? It was not just a few, not a select group; it was ALL the assembled worshipers. So I am reminded that I have a job at church when others are up front serving, not to observe, but to participate.

Church is not a spectator sport, neither is it sitting on the bench. It is rather getting on the field, getting in the ring, actually jumping into the shopping fray to find the deal. We are not called to sit. We are called to participate. I just wonder what God would do if all the assembled worshipers at our churches would plead with Him to move in our midst.

Day 4

Yes, Black Friday is an adventure. Sometimes it's exciting, thrilling, exhilarating, finding just the best deal. Sometimes it feels a lot like walking into a deep dark jungle with the chance of being swallowed by some horrible monster. It can be really scary when people are diving into boxes head first (honestly, it was a sale on pillows) or grabbing blindly. But sometimes BLACK Friday can turn GOLDEN.

And so it was on this Black Friday. We had gotten the ads and scoured over them. My nieces are bargain hunters through and through, so they created the plan of attack. We would start at the shoe store at about 4:00 AM because they were giving $10.00 off coupons for the first one hundred people in the line. So there we were. The temperature was just a little over zero degrees. My nieces were at the front of the line and my sisters and I were back somewhere in the fifty to sixty person range. It was disconcerting to see people getting out of their cars to join their friends who were holding places in front of us. Would we get the discount?

Sometime after about an hour of shivering, (where's a hot flash when you want one?) the store doors opened and we received the coupons. But coupons were not the only part of the promotion, this store also had huge cash give-a-ways.

I want you to understand the excitement when you're handed a ticket and you know they are going to call a "winning" number. We had done this before because each year they give away prizes, cash, coupons. Oh my, it makes my budget conscious brain swim. The first give-away was at six and it was for a cash prize. This was worth staying for. After each of us used our precious coupons and bought some on sale, deal-of-the-century boots, we waited. They were offering doughnuts, but sugar can fog the brain and we had to stay focused. It was only 6:00 AM and we had deals to find.

Finally the time came and the number was called. A woman screamed, waved the ticket, did a little dance, she had won the money. We deposited our non-winning tickets in the trash and went to Target. But we could echo the words of the Terminator, "We'll be back". The next cash give-away was at 8:00. This was calculated down to seconds so we could still shop at other stores and yet be back at just the right time for the next big prize.

At about 7:58 we reentered. Tickets were being passed out and we were laughing, enjoying the process. The anticipation of winning is half the fun, especially when we're together. At eight o'clock a man rose to the top of a very tall ladder asking everyone to look at their tickets.

"Does anyone here want to win some money?"

"Yes" we all joined our voices into one.

He called the winning sequence of numbers. Everyone in the crowd had the same first, second, and third numbers so there was lots of yelling. By about the sixth number, voices were lessening and you could hear disappointment, "Awwwe".

But I was still in the running. Suddenly a quiet calm came over me. I looked at my ticket. He was calling numbers one at a time to draw out the excitement. Before he ever called the last three digits, I knew...I just knew...I had it. When he called the last number, I didn't scream, I didn't react in any unusual way except to begin to walk forward. My niece was surprised and even asked why I was moving. I walked up to the man and said, "I have it". He smiled.

The Prize? A thousand dollars. Now let me say that again, ONE THOUSAND DOLLARS. After signing papers, they handed me ten crisp, new, one hundred dollar bills and we exited. After doing some quick tax figuring we divided the money among the six of us and each went home that day with more money than we started with. Not a bad way to start Christmas shopping.

Yes, Black Friday had turned "golden". But that was by no means the end of this story. God had a much bigger, more golden plan for doing this than mere money, just as He always has with each blessing.

Luke 1

The book of Luke records in 1:7 that Zechariah
and Elizabeth were well along in years. Isn't that a
lovely way to say old? We could also say they were
in their golden years. How old? We don't know, but
too old to have a child. So what did Elizabeth think
over the last years? Did she look at herself in the
bathroom mirror and say "I'm not young enough.
I'm not able to have a child, I'm not..."

What is the voice you hear? "I'm not talented
enough. I'm not smart enough. I'm not good looking enough. I'm not old enough. I'm not young
enough. I AM NOT..."

The place of "I am not" is a very dark world to live
in. But do you remember that this is the Christmas
story? Nearly everyone you will meet in this story in
Luke begins in those shadows. But where I am not,
He is. It is no accident that one of His names is I AM.

We are going to see His beautiful Christmas lights
in each life. He wants to take the darkness and turn
it into gold. Why not look for those lights of gold in
your life?

Day 5

"Not a creature was stirring, not even a mouse."

Really? That hasn't been my experience. Mice "stir" all the time. They know it is the season, pull out their wooden spoons and off they go stirring up trouble wherever their little legs take them. Let me share some stories:

One of my friends was in the kitchen when her husband decided to make a piece of toast. He pulled out the toaster. That is a pretty mundane thing to do but it didn't stay that way for long. Suddenly a mouse jumped to freedom. He hadn't been stirring either until things started to heat up. But there he was. He didn't stay to chat. He just wanted to leave his calling card.

Another friend was driving when one came leaping out of the car's vent into her lap.

Are you getting that? A MOUSE JUMPED OUT OF THE VENT! I think she wrecked the car.

Things start breaking in my brain when I even think about it. If this would have happened to me, I would never have been right again.

There is another story tucked way back in my memory that takes the cake, well actually the cookies. It was the holiday season and our mom had just put the finishing touches on the COOKIES, covered them with a cloth so the icing could set and went off to bed.

What she didn't know was that a party had been called and she was not invited. The resident mice began to stir...all over those holiday cookies. Now doesn't that sound yummy!

Mom saw the evidence the next day. Things like that are what give mice their bad name.

And it isn't like you can salvage any of the cookies. It would ruin the idea of chocolate sprinkles in the hearts and lives of children everywhere.

Mice don't stir? I hate to have to be the one to break this to you but they got that part of the story wrong.

Luke 1

My house is quiet, so even the smallest noise seems loud against the silence. No one is stirring, and on this day, not even mice.

My friend Zechariah in Luke 1:5-17 went into the stillness of the Temple. This was the biggest day of his life, but what Zechariah did not know, was that it was about to get so much bigger. That quiet stillness was broken by a message from God Himself, delivered by the angel Gabriel. Zechariah's prayer had been heard, and the answer was on the way.

This is one of the reasons I so love to study the Scripture. I never know when God Himself will break through the silence and speak a special message just to me.

Day 6

And then there was Mr. Jing-A-Ling. Never heard of him? Oh my, you missed it. He wasn't quite on the level of Santa Claus but he was a close second. He lived inside of our TV, surrounded by props that were probably made of cardboard. He hosted a very short little program that began the countdown to the Christmas season at our house. Although, if the truth be told, that countdown began in my heart every December 27th, the saddest day of the year. The 26th was still good because we got to stay in our pajamas all day, play with our toys, and drink hot chocolate with a candy cane melting into it.

Was the program national? I don't think so. Were there any special effects? Well, yes, he sat in a chair and talked about Christmas. We thought that was about as special as you could ever hope to witness. And then there was the music. How many years ago was it that I was privileged to hear those notes as they announced that Christmas was coming? Longer than I care to mention.

I know this, the music was magical. Even after so many Christmas seasons have passed, my sisters and I could still sing you the song that filled our TV room as these notes transported us into another room, the Christmas room of imagination. It ranked right up there with putting up the Christmas tree, the last day of school as Christmas break began, and the arrival of the Sears' Wish Book. As soon as that showed up, we sprawled out on the carpet and thumbed as quickly as we could past the clothes to the good stuff, dolls, doll houses, games, puzzles, bikes. It was a world that we only entered at Christmas time.

We grew up in a time when most of the toys we had were outside in our back yard. Our play house was a creek, where you could catch minnows and frogs. We made pretend brooms out of sticks and "soap" out of the silt at the bottom of the creek. If I had only known the beauty of mud facials at that time, today I would be the CEO of my own company. (Can you tell that I still live in a world of imagination?)

Mr. Jing-a-Ling had a big job to do. He was there to tell us that something special was about to happen. Christmas was coming.

Luke 1

What a job Gabriel had, showing up, surprising ordinary folks with absolutely extraordinary, exciting, earth shaking news. For Zechariah, it was a child born when the season had long since passed. For Mary it was an impossible birth with no earthly father.

It sure sounds like Gabriel had a fun job. But he gave this description to Zechariah in Luke 1:19, *"I stand in the presence of God and I have been sent to speak to you and tell you this good news."* That was what Gabriel did on a regular basis. He stood near God. All the beauty, all the joy, all the delight of the ages was right there in God's presence. And while I am sure he was honored to obey the Lord and come and share this good news with humans, it meant leaving the glorious presence of God in Heaven. Someday, some wonderful day, this same privilege will be ours to just gloriously dwell in His presence. No wonder the angels sing.

Day 7

It's hard to make a name for yourself in the culinary world when you come from a family of cooks.

But I have.

That is evident when my sisters, kids, and I bake Christmas cookies.

Now, I have to set the background for this. We don't just bake chocolate chip and peanut butter. Oh no. We bake at least twenty different kinds. And not one of them is decorated the same way. There are sprinkles on the iced ones and icing on the sprinkled ones. Christmas trees have garland and cinnamon candies to look like holly berries and snow. Some of these creations are dipped in chocolate and some of the chocolate is dipped in more chocolate.

Are you getting the picture? These are not cookies. These are COOKIES. There is such a sugary mist hanging in the air, that you can gain weight just by breathing.

It is a Christmas tradition to do this. It takes much more than a day and then they are divided up among all of us.

Many of our families put this on their calendar and think about it for months. It becomes a destination event in the home of the sister who has the largest kitchen. That means it is never in my kitchen. I am okay with that!

But over the years a pecking order has emerged to make sure the job is done with the utmost care, precision, efficiency, and artistic expression. There's the varsity team, the reserve team, and the bench warmers. After all you can't let just anyone work on COOKIES.

I should know. I have moved up to a very special job. They now let me shake the sprinkles!

I told you that I have made a name for myself in the culinary world. Mine comes from the Dutch word for sprinkles. It is "hagelslag."

So there you have it. When I arrive on the cookie baking day, a whisper circles the table. I think they are saying, "It's good old Hagelslag."

But there is another name that I am striving for. It is a level above where I am now. It is the German name for a cinnamon star Christmas cookie. It is "zimtsterne".

But don't hold your breath. Everybody thinks "Hagelslag" fits pretty well.

Luke 1

I love Christmas, all the syrupy, sugary, sweet tastes and tales of Christmas. I love the movies with snow swirling on the screen, even if it isn't snowing outside. I love the lights twinkling and trees glowing. I even love the old children's Christmas shows like "The Grinch" and "Rudolph".

However, I get very tired of the theme that runs through some of the programs: "Believe, just believe". You see it isn't enough to just believe. Our belief has to be in God and in what He says. What we believe matters.

Zechariah couldn't quite come to grips with God doing the impossible. Zechariah couldn't quite wrap his mind around God's plan. In Luke 1:18 he asked the angel Gabriel, *"How can I be sure of this, I am an old man and my wife is well along in years?"* God gave him nine months to quietly think about it.

Day 8

It was a hard time. My heart was broken. My life appeared to be in shambles. Sometimes I was swallowed up in grief. I was alone and felt that aloneness not only around me but also deep inside of me.

I had always loved music, was a singer most of my life, but at this point the song was gone. It had been stripped out by the pain. Even as I sat in church with praise music lifted up, I was having a hard time finding the music since life seemed so bleak.

And so it was when one evening I was watching a Christian television program, a group was singing a song about heaven. I stopped for a moment and just breathed a few words, "God, when will I ever sing again?" That was it, just a simple question and at that point in my life. I was not even completely sure that God heard me because the grief was so big. It encompassed everything else. But He did and He does, even when we feel so small or far away.

Just a few minutes later the phone rang. Now let me reiterate, no one had heard my prayer except God. I was home alone. But God is the only one who needs to hear the cries of our hearts. It is enough for the One who never sleeps, to hear. In the midst of disappointment, or sorrow, or despair, or such grief that it swallows us, He can let us know in miraculous ways that He hears. The voice on the other end of the line was a woman I had known some years before. I had not seen her for some time. She identified herself and then told me she had a message for me. She said, "A little while ago I felt like I should call you to tell you something. God told me to tell you, it's time for you to sing again."

I haltingly thanked her but was almost too stunned to speak. Hadn't I just asked that? Hadn't I just whispered those simple words? God answered. And He answered so quickly that I knew He was putting the song back into my broken heart. But it was more than the song, it was a confirmation that God does hear, no matter how broken or alone we are.

He is there and He hears our prayers immediately even if the answers come later on. You see He is the giver and restorer of the song and the listener to every prayer.

Luke 1

In Luke 1:13 Zechariah was in the temple and heard the first recorded revelation from God in over 400 years. The angel Gabriel broke the silence with these words, *"Do not be afraid, Zechariah, your prayer has been heard."*

What was Zechariah's prayer? Was it the prayer that was on the lips of every Israelite, that God would redeem Israel? Or was it the more personal prayer that he had prayed over and over in his marriage, that God would give them a child?

I will admit I don't understand how prayer works, but what I love, is that if his prayer was national or personal, the answer was still the same. The God of the Universe had heard and the answer was on the way. Today, as I pray about national and personal issues, I can rest in this, God has heard my prayer and I need not be afraid.

During this Christmas season, have you lost your song? Is there a very personal prayer or do world events hang heavy on your heart? Know this... God hears.

Day 9

For many people 4:00 AM is not the beginning of
the day but rather the middle of the night. But I
love this time before the sun kisses the sky and I
see the first glimmer of an amber blush streaking
across the horizon.

Most often, it means I am sitting on my couch, a
Bible (or some electronic version) on my lap, a cup
of coffee in my hand and a pen nearby. I am spending some quiet time before a very loud day.
But this silent night is not quite silent. There is the
whisper of a song. It began before time and one day
pierced my heart with its message of hope and grace.

I was introduced to Jesus when I was fourteen. I
had known about the Christmas baby. But then I
met The Easter Lord and Savior.

This song is a very unusual type of music. It has
been written, not to accompany my voice, but to accompany my life.

Someone told me one day that I sail through life...
no pain, no heartache, no big problems. It might
look that way but it has never been the reality.
When I had been married less than two years, my
husband and I were given the news that we could

not have children. No matter what tone you try to put with that, even if you make it the ring tone on your phone, it means a visit to the Heartbreak Hotel. (Okay, let's back up the train. First of all, I am not old enough to have witnessed the debut of that song. Secondly, it is by no means my favorite genre. And thirdly, the lyrics do not fit my circumstance but the title does. And when you hear the news about infertility, you do make reservations "at the end of Lonely Street". So in spite of any objections my sisters might raise as we write this, I am using that phrase!)

I cried. I hurt. I wanted to become a mom. I had already figured out how my life was going to go. We would be married a little over two years and have a son. Two years later, we would have another son and when we reached four boys, we would stop. Doesn't that sound organized? Doesn't it sound neat and clean?

But the path that Jesus puts us on is usually not that easy to walk. Often there are some pretty messy circumstances that we have to face.

I am not going to take you down the path through the years of waiting. It is too much information. But I will say that I didn't walk around with my head to my chest. I didn't wear sackcloth.

Yes, there were tears and words of impatience as the months stretched into years, but Jesus offers rivers of delight and the light of His Word made me see peace.

Finally though, one Tuesday afternoon in June, the telephone rang and the voice at the other end said, "Congratulations, you have a two month old baby girl!"

No matter how many times I tell this story, no matter how hard I try to give it a voice that is not so emotional, I can't. It was a miracle day and I can't tell it any other way. It can only be compared to a day three years later when I heard the voice of our case worker tell me that this time we had a nine day old son!

God's plan for our children had been completed. The waiting was over. We had a beautiful little girl and an energetic little boy. I hadn't known it, but they had been mine since before time began. It has been my joy and crown to call them my children. It became quite clear to me that Jesus had chosen us to be a parable to those watching of how we can be adopted into His family.

Their little voices had always been the melody to that music God had orchestrated for my life. I just hadn't been able to hear it.

By the way, years later at three o'clock AM, on a very cold January day, the telephone rang. My son announced that they had just given birth to their second child. That meant they now had two sons. My daughter already had two little boys.

For me, that meant we had four grandsons. It was at that moment that I realized that I now had my four little boys!

That had always been God's plan for me. I had just been a generation off.

Yes, the waiting was over!

Luke 1

Part of my prayer has come from Luke 11:1, *"Lord, teach me to pray."* It is so simple, but God has made me stop when Scripture speaks of prayer and linger over the passage.

That's what I am doing with Zechariah's prayer. How many years had he and Elizabeth prayed for a child? How many months were their hopes dashed? Why did God not answer?

We know from verse 25 that at least Elizabeth felt the disgrace of God's supposed silence on the matter. Now it was no longer possible for them to have a child. Had they stopped praying for it? Had they resigned themselves to the inevitable?

And yet God's plan was right there, right now. They were to be a part of a miracle. It took an angel to deliver the news and even then Zechariah didn't believe. (I love him!) So waiting is a part of prayer. Asking over and over is part of it too. Even the part when it is no longer possible, is part of it.

Perhaps those prayers I've prayed for years will involve me in a miracle. What I know for sure is that I can trust a God who can make the impossible, possible.

Day 10

I had such good intentions. I had the meals planned and the time figured. I went to the grocery and picked up the exact ingredients.

I was set. The Christmas season is busy so I had the crock pot ready. Set on low. Filled with good-for-you vegetables and meat. Done when I got home! I had this!

But I came home and to my surprise, dinner was not ready...figured the time wrong again. Oh well, I was still ahead. I could fix a peanut butter and jelly sandwich. We hadn't had that for a little while. I would have dinner fixed for tomorrow. I would just cook it a little longer.

But as it turned out, a little longer turned into a lot. Maybe all those flavors melded together. (What does that mean anyway?) It would still be good, and soft, with just the right amount of dryness. (I threw that one in just to make sure you were paying attention.) You know, a hot stew on a very cold night.

My husband tried. He really did. But I knew when I saw his plate.

I apologized and told him that I would eat it. I hate

to waste food. I grew up with the host of starving children that needed the food I refused to eat. He was very gracious and choked down most of what I made, but his response just consisted of three little words.

I know what you're thinking. "I love you." Not at all! Instead I heard..."Don't torture yourself!"

Oh, the sting of disgrace.

But if you happen to be out, feel free to come over, we have leftovers.

The Recipe
2 LARGE turkey thighs
Carrots
Potatoes
Crock pot
Cook for at least 37 hours and
Test for doneness (the right amount of dryness)
Serves 100 (no one eats much)

Luke 1

Luke 1:25 says that Elizabeth felt the sting of disgrace among the people for her barrenness. People assumed that if you didn't have a child, it was God's disfavor on your life. But the truth from Scripture is that sometimes there was a season of waiting before God gave the children who would be used greatly. Abraham and Sarah heard the promise but had to wait many years for Isaac. Isaac and Rebecca waited twenty years for Jacob and Esau. Jacob and Rachel waited for Joseph. And Elkanah and Hannah waited a long time before they had Samuel.

The waiting wasn't easy. Their cradles were empty, their eyes would have dripped with tears at times, no little feet romped through their homes. But God did the miraculous and once again we are reminded of this. Zechariah and Elizabeth waited until it was absolutely impossible for them to have a child. But God renewed their aged bodies. He took what was barren and made it fruitful. God took the dead part and breathed life. Their hearts rejoiced because not only would they bear a child, but they knew God had done it. He had shone His favor. He had taken away the disgrace.

I bear the sting of disgrace for my own sinfulness, but God has done the miraculous. He sent the Savior and because of Him, God has made my life new. He has taken death and replaced it with life. He has taken away my disgrace and made fruitful that which was barren. With tears of gratitude I will sing with Elizabeth, *"The Lord has done this for me...He has shone His favor."*

Day 11

I'm going to open the door and invite you into my home. Most of the time my house is brown, brown wood, brown furniture, brown carpet. Yeah, pretty much brown. Now don't get me wrong, it's not just one shade of brown, but rather the brown family. I do, though, add color to the walls. I have coffee colored walls, hot chocolate colored walls and pecan colored walls. Oh wait, I guess that is all still brown. My carpet is the color of dirt so it doesn't show the dirt. It's every woman's dream. I do add pops of color by adding pillows of harvest gold and burnt umber. Let's face it there's not a lot of blue, pink or purple at my house.

By the end of October I'm a little tired of brown and maybe even a little tired of the fall decorations that have been out since July, so it's time to be thinking about Christmas. Finally the day of the transformation arrives. I go to the closet and grab. I blow away a year's worth of dust from the top of each box. I pull out the hangers for the stockings, ornaments that the children and grandchildren have made, lights, greenery, wreathes, last year's 90% off bargains...Oh I forgot I got that one...and of course the Christmas tree. It's all work, but it is such fun work. I clean as I go so and everything gets a Christmas face lift. It's a shot of North Pole botox.

Wrinkles from the stretched carpet disappear under a Christmas rug. The scar on the front door is hidden by the lighted wreath. When it's all finished I stand back. Lights are twinkling, greenery dusted with snow covers the mantle, and the Christmas tree sends out a warm holiday greeting to passers-by. The house is transformed from the ordinary to the extraordinary.

The North Pole Christmas Village has come to dwell among the brown mundane for the weeks ahead.

Luke 1

In Luke 1:26 we are introduced to Mary, an ordinary girl, from an ordinary town, with an ordinary life. What she doesn't know is that the ordinary is about to become the extraordinary, the mundane, the miraculous.

The brown dusty streets of her village are suddenly illuminated by an angel visit. Gabriel is delivering a message from God that will change her young life.

The Christmas story began in the heart of God before the foundation of the world. But at that very moment, it began for Mary. The Messiah, the Savior was coming. Can you imagine how she must have felt? This had never before taken place. The God of the Universe would come to dwell in her. Her life was about to be transformed.

And that is STILL the Christmas story. Jesus came to transform us. At this very moment it can begin for you. The God of the Universe wants to come and dwell in your life.

Day 12

In the summer of my sixth grade year the Christmas anticipation began to build exponentially. Three boys, who had just moved into the area, came riding into my life. Please understand, it was not the three boys. Oh, they were nice enough, even kind for teenage boys, but what I fell in love with were their chariots of fire. They each had a fiery red bicycle. I had never ridden a bike before. I had never experienced the wind blowing through my hair, or the power beneath me as I flew down a hill, or the feeling of pride as I was able to manipulate the two wheels. A portal opened, and once through, I could not go back. The bicycle became the epitome of exquisiteness, the pinnacle of perfection, the embodiment of excellence (no mere mundane words could describe my overwhelming love for this mode of transportation). I WANTED A BIKE!

So my Christmas list began and ended with one word...bike. When asked, "What do you want for Christmas?" the answer was simple, "A bike". When looking through the Wish Book, the dog-eared pages were the ones with the bikes.

School began. Thanksgiving came and went. The short December days crawled by, but with each day the anticipation, the desire, the hope grew. In all of the years past, looking forward to Christmas meant mystery, the unknown gifts, but this year it was the hope of one...a bike.

Christmas day arrived. Finally, in those early pre-dawn hours when darkness was turning to light, my brothers and sisters and I were allowed entrance into the living room where our presents awaited.

I looked, but there were no boxes big enough to house a bicycle. That wasn't unusual because our parents often hid gifts. I opened the boxes and found gloves, a game and some new pajamas. Then I waited and waited and waited...nothing more.

The hope of a bike was over.

I tried so hard not to cry.

Luke 1

Part of the beauty of Christmas is the wait, the anticipation, the excitement of looking forward. How appropriate for this season.

When Adam and Eve sinned way back in Genesis 3, right there in the midst of their sin, God promised that the seed of the woman would crush the head of the serpent. And so began the promise of the Christmas story. The promise was given and Adam and Eve waited. God told Abraham that the blessing would come through him and Abraham waited. The prophets foretold His birth, and the world waited.

But here in Luke 1:30-33, the wait is finally over. His name is Jesus, Savior, The Son of the Most High.

Day 13

Hey, remember Black Friday and the thousand dollars? I walked away that day feeling so amazingly blessed, so loved and cherished that God would pour out His sweet favor. It was a reminder that we belong to Him and He takes very good care of us. But as I reflect back over how God used that, I am even more reminded of His greatness.

Some time ago I joined my sisters and their husbands on a tour that my bother-in-law was leading to Israel. This would be my first time. They had already been twice before and had talked about the joy of being there, learning and experiencing the Holy Land, the place where Jesus walked. I was excited. I drove the 100+ miles to spend the night with my sister since we were flying out early the next day from their city. I had carefully packed, prepared to be gone the ten days, and left enough room to bring home treasures. Yes, I was ready. I had a hard time sleeping, first because I was so excited and secondly because we had to rise so early. I was afraid I would over sleep so I just couldn't sleep at all.

Finally I got up. It was about 1:00 AM and I simply could not stay in bed any longer. I determined that I would be as quiet as I could so I didn't wake them but soon there was a knock on the door. It was my brother-in-law telling me that the trip was cancelled for that morning and we would NOT be leaving. I thought he was kidding. He was not. The connecting flight into Chicago had been cancelled because of bad weather. By that time all of us were up to try to get the whole thing figured out. In the morning the airline gave him the plan. Some of the tour people would be leaving later that day and some would have to go the next day.

I was part of the "next day" group. No discussion, no recourse, no other plan and no refund. The airline made the decision who would go and who would stay. My brother-in-law was leading the group so he and my sister were on the first round. My other sister, her husband and I were on the second, along with about ten more people. I remember asking the Lord about this. I could not quite understand since I had never been how it was "fair" that I was missing a day. But this only reminds me, that when our plans are changed, to look for His plan... the one that might have some "gold" lining.

Finally the next morning we boarded the very small plane to Chicago. As I looked I noticed a rather nice looking, about my age, gentleman sitting in the seat next to mine. Very quickly I prayed, "Now Lord, I know the schedule was changed for a reason so this man is either going to be my husband (I'm single) or you want me to tell him about You."

I sat down and smiled. We began to chat about where we were going and just exchange reasons for our trips. About fifteen seconds into the conversation I knew he was NOT going to be my husband so God must have a divine appointment lined up. I was excited.

He told me in words that were pretty graphic that he was NOT happy about going to Chicago. He had to go for work.

"Really, where do you work?" I asked.

"I'm an executive with _____." And he named the shoe store where I had won the thousand dollars. ARE YOU KIDDING ME?!!!! (Do you get the connection? I had a story to tell him so now I had a way in.) I smiled. "Oh, let me tell you about your store!" He stiffened. I could see it all over him. He must have thought he was sitting next to a woman who was going to give him an earful about some pair of shoes that fell apart within days, or shoes that squeaked horribly when she walked, or about some employee who was rude and obnoxious.

I said, "Oh no, this is a good thing." I proceeded to tell him the story of the thousand dollars and what a blessing it was.

He relaxed and began to open up. He had recently separated from his wife. He was broken and sad and desperately needed something, "a new direction in his life" he said.

I began to talk to him about how Jesus could give him that new direction. He was skeptical. He tapped on the shoulder of the woman sitting diagonally in front of him. "Do you hear what she is saying...this is crazy talk isn't it?"

Now let me remind you that there were other Israel tour people on the plane and this was one of them. Beth turned around and said, "No, she's telling you the truth, listen to her."

He listened a little more, then turned around to the person directly behind him, "Do you hear what this woman is saying? This is crazy isn't it?" Jamie (Yep, more Israel tour people.) smiled and said, "You need to listen. She's telling you the truth."

He was surrounded. Those who were too far away were praying (like my sister) because it was such a small plane and they could hear.

Are you getting the scope of this? God had set it all up. A year and a half before, I had won the money from his company which gave me an open door. Our plane had been delayed by one day so that a team of us would be with and around this man. I had been through a terrible, heartbreaking separation and divorce so I could identify with his pain.

And yet, I could still tell this man of the loveliness of God and how He had a plan for him and a new direction.

I said, "You know, God must love you a whole lot to have rearranged the schedules of all of these people, so we could be on the plane with you today to tell you about Jesus." He listened and before the plane landed he prayed with me to ask Jesus to be his Savior.

Now how about that for a GOLDEN ending! You see all of us are highly favored by the Lord. He loves us so much that He arranges for each of us to have divine appointments. He wants each of us to come to know Him as Savior and Lord. Maybe today is your time.

Luke 1

In Luke 1:28 the angel Gabriel told Mary that she was highly favored. So what did the divine favor look like in her life? Mary experienced a miracle so great that it had never before happened on the planet. She carried the Child of God. The absolutely impossible had become possible.

But it also meant that people would whisper about her reputation, eyebrows would be raised when her name was mentioned. Even Joseph was going to need divine intervention so he could believe. But Mary knew the truth, and she was the Lord's servant. That was enough.

Mary was the first to "receive" the Savior. She became His mother. We have the opportunity to receive Him as our Savior and then God becomes our Father.

Day 14

How do you know if someone loves you? Let me give you a couple of clues that pretty much cover it. Almost everyone falls into one of these categories when it comes to interpreting if someone loves them. Keep this in mind when you are Christmas shopping:

Time
Words
Actions
Touch
Gifts

For me, it is actions. If you love me, you will help me clean the house or take out the trash, or fold the laundry...that is a big one!

Now stay with me. I am going to tell you a story that was a convincing proof to me that Jesus loves me. I get altitude sickness, no, not the kind that requires me to lease a hyperbaric chamber. My altitude sickness doesn't make my brain swell. My smart aleck nephew tells me that wouldn't be a problem anyway because I have such a tiny brain and he has a big brain. (Guess who's not inheriting anything from me.)

All I really need to do is drink a lot of water. Since I don't want a raging headache, flu like symptoms, or something that resembles carbon monoxide poisoning, I drink a lot of water.

Okay, that's not a big deal. It's cheap. It's doable. It doesn't taste bad.

We were in Montana and were heading toward Jackson Hole, Wyoming. I got up, ate breakfast in the hotel and gulped as much water as I could choke down. I combined that with a couple of cups of coffee and got in the car.

The name Montana comes from a Native American word that means "big sky." What a beautiful, peaceful, restful word for a breathtaking state. But "big sky" means you see the sky and not a lot of anything else, including bathrooms. (By the way, I'm the sister with the bad cooking stories and another gut wrenching, mortifying bathroom story I'll tell you about later. I'm a mess!)

We were on the road about fifteen minutes when it hit me. We had already driven outside of civilization when I made it known that I would like to stop. Everybody said that would be okay and we would stop at the next place. When I first mentioned this, it was not at critical mass, it was simply a request.

Most of the time bathroom stops are pretty convenient, but it soon became apparent that this stop was not going to be convenient.

Finally, we found a gas station. We pulled in. It was a shack, but to me, it looked beautiful. I thought I heard angels singing. Miserably, it was not only closed, it was abandoned. That place is permanently etched into my brain and, according to my nephew, it made my brain even smaller. It was at the edge of the world's end. I knew I was doomed. I could identify with Mary when she was told there was no room in the inn and her water was about to break. That much water in anybody's system has to escape. First you begin to perspire, hands sweating profusely, you wipe your brow. Then it comes out as tears. But it has little hope of going anywhere else, unless you packed the Depends.

We drove on. At this point I wasn't the only one looking for a bathroom. Everyone in the car was helping me search. Anything would do. I was praying. I think everybody was. The ramifications of a trip all the way to Jackson Hole with me screaming for a bathroom, only to be followed by the whisper "Never mind," was almost too much to think about. It made everyone's brain get a little smaller.

At this point I had given up the hope of an actual bathroom. I have to be perfectly honest, I have no idea what came over me, I'm pretty sure I had water on the brain. I spied a low-to-the ground road sign. I prayed that there could possibly be an outhouse behind it. I would have kissed the half-moon on the door if there had been.

But there wasn't...THERE WASN'T!

But sometimes our finite brains, flooded with fears, anxiety and pain, or even too much liquid, don't ask enough of our infinite God, whose giving is so much bigger than our asking.

And then suddenly my heart wanted to sing. There it was, gleaning in the morning sun, a PORTA-JOHN®! There it was right out there in big sky country. I still think that the Lord dropped it out of the clouds just for me. I knew I would never look at a Porta-John® the same way again. I had asked for an outhouse. He gave me more than I asked for.

So what did that say to me? It said that God loves me. That He cares about the very big things in my life and He cares about the very little things.

This was a miracle for me and that action said "I love you".

Luke 1

Luke 1 is filled with miracles. Zechariah saw the angel Gabriel and Zechariah's silence spoke volumes. He and Elizabeth were about to deliver a miracle child and her growing womb gave testimony to God's amazing favor. Then Mary came to their home with the secret she carried. The unborn child John leaped at the coming of the Messiah. Elizabeth, filled with the Spirit of God, testified of God's greatness. This was a season of miracles, but it didn't end with them.

Because I hold in my hands the Word of God, I can experience their joy and amazement and awe at God's greatness. I can burst into song right along with Mary. *"My soul glorifies the Lord and my spirit rejoices in God my Savior."*

Day 15

Have you ever wanted to write a song? I have and have had visions of penning something so wonderful that it rivaled Bach, Mozart, Elvis or the Beatles. These people have been called world changers. Now I want you to understand no one asked me to do this. Yet it burned inside of me to write something that would echo through the years. And it has. Oh, you haven't heard it? Let me share it with you?

Johnny was my steady
Three months ago
He had to join the army
I begged him not to go
He said it was his duty
He wouldn't be there long
He had to go and fight the war
Right or wrong

Why did they take you Johnny (sung Jaa Haa
Neee with great sadness)
Take you so very far away
When they knew how much I loved you (sung La-
Uhved you, again with even more sadness)
And how I wanted you to stay

I still wear his ring
On a chain around my neck
I think about him day and night
And wish he would come back

Now I could go on, but it's obvious that the gut-wrenching pathos of the song is too much for the Christmas season.

As I reflect on the absolute stupidity of these words, I wonder, "What was I thinking?" Who was it in the government who knew that I loved Jaa Haa Nee and how on earth did they find it out? You see, when this song was written, it was long before internet spying. Nevertheless, I wanted a song that would live on, and live on it has...at family gatherings, at Christmas, during the playing of charades, sung in whispered tones, shouted across parking lots, danced to and may even be the ring tone on my sister's phone because she will NOT let it die.

Now I realize that I have left you at the edge of a cliff hanger by not completing the song. So let me tell you how it ends so you can sleep tonight. Johnny never came back...I wish he would have taken the song with him.

Luke 1

So again, have you ever wished that you could write beautiful music? As I already said, I have. There are songs that bring me to tears, some express just how my heart feels, some dance around in my head for days and one brings utter embarrassment. Mary's heart was so full. She had to express it. Luke 1:46-55 records her worship, her praise, her song of joy.

While I may not be able to write such a song, I can most certainly join my voice with hers in praise and worship of our great God.

Day 16

Let me go back to that sixth grade Christmas. The hope of the bike was over. I tried so hard not to cry. Perhaps in a few months for my birthday I could hope again. But there was never much money for birthdays and that was the reason that some Christmases had only few gifts.

In a family of six children there was little money for extras. I understood it, but it was still painful and the disappointment was still great. Tears, first one, then another, I kept telling myself not to cry. Yet tears started streaming down my face.

My brother and I were told to gather up the wrapping paper and take it downstairs to the fireplace in the basement. Carrying the torn paper was a reminder that the gifts were over. The weight of the paper was light but it weighed heavily on my heart. My parents knew that doing something might help me to calm down a little. I thought I could cry downstairs in private. All those months of waiting and now the hope was going to be tossed into the fireplace with the torn Christmas wrapping paper.

I did not move quickly down the stairs to the basement; disappointment slows your steps. But sometimes "suddenlies" break through disappointment and pain. About half way down the stairs I looked over to the basement floor and there gleaming in the sunshine were five bicycles and a small push-pedal car. I couldn't move, I could barely breathe. The dream that had died was now resurrected and "suddenly" it was CHRISTMAS!

Luke 1

In Luke 1:57-80, Zechariah had endured nine months of waiting, not being able to speak. An incredible miracle had happened to him in the Temple and he couldn't even tell people about it. Now on the eighth day after his son's birth, everyone assumed Zechariah and Elizabeth would name him after his father. Elizabeth said the name was John, but everyone insisted there were no relatives by that name. Zechariah communicated his need for a tablet and wrote four little words. *"His name is John."*

Suddenly Zechariah's mouth was opened, his tongue was loosed, and he began to speak. After nine months of silence, his first words were praise to God. He had been waiting nine months, not to tell his own story, but to praise the God who did it all.

Day 17

Take a deep breath. It is Christmas in Yellowstone. In some places the air is filled with diamond dust. Buffalo, elk, and moose dot the fields and Old Faithful looks as if it was a cloud of silver. Mountains lift their majestic heads as far as you can see. Outside of the park there is one of the most charming cities in the United States. It is Jackson Hole, Wyoming. There is an elk horn archway into a small park area. The crowd holds their breath as a countdown is about to end. Suddenly the night sky is filled with the soft glow of lights that are nestled beneath a blanket of new snow and the silence ends as applause and laughter explode in this little canyon at the foot of those starry mountains.

Doesn't it sound like a wonderful destination? Have you ever been there? I have, but not at Christmas. Would I love to see it? Yes. And maybe someday I will, but not this year.

This year there will be diamond dust in the eyes of my little grandchildren who will open gifts at my house. There will be a cloud of silver as the wrapping paper is torn off and tossed into the sir. The buffalo and elk sit on a bench at my house. I purchased them on one of my trips so those little ones could play with them.

Is there a countdown? Yes, but I am the only one who hears it. It ends when the doorbell rings and the silence is filled with the laughter that explodes as these little people run into my family room. No majestic mountains to lift their heads but rather majestic little faces lift their eyes.

I realize that not everyone gets to experience Christmas the way I do. But as remarkable as those moments are, they pale in comparison to another Christmas destination.

It is found within the pages of the most majestic Book ever written. Open your Bibles to Luke chapter 2. A countdown is about to end. This one began before time. Sheep dot the fields and diamond dust fills the air.

Take a deep breath.

It is Christmas in Bethlehem.

Luke 2

"O Little Town of Bethlehem"...it really is a little town, even today. I have had the joy of walking down its streets, standing on its hillside, seeing with my own eyes this renown place. But the very first time I was there, what spoke so loudly to me, was that this place would have little significance except for one thing, Jesus Christ was born there. His presence made all the difference.

"In those days Caesar Augustus issued a decree that a census should be taken of the entire Roman world. (This was the first census that took place while Quirinius was governor of Syria.) And everyone went to their own town to register.

So Joseph also went up from the town of Nazareth in Galilee to Judea, to Bethlehem, the town of David because he belonged to the house and line of David."
Luke 2:1-4

If His birth can make a difference in a little town, just think what He can do with a life.

Day 18

Shopping can really be fun: the exhilaration of the
hunt, the joy of the pursuit, the rush you get with
the perfect find. But Christmas shopping, well let's
be honest, it can be taxing, at least sometimes it's
that way for me. I went to the store with the 25%
off coupon, I found the perfect gift, and stood in
line until I thought my bladder might actually burst
(remember I have coffee each morning) just to hear
the sales person say, "Oh, I'm so sorry, that coupon
is not good on this item."

I looked once again at the coupon and it clearly said
25% off. I looked at the name of the store and yes,
that was the store where I was shopping. Then with
squinted eyes I read the fine print...good only on
potato mashers. And here I had been trying to buy
the perfect coffee maker. So I walked back out of
the line. But remember, I had this bursting bladder
because I had stood in line waiting to find out that
the coupon was no good, and I had had coffee.

After asking directions to the ladies room I finally
saw it. It was the one with the line three miles long.
I stood in line again and waited. Finally my turn
came. It was a good thing too because remember
I had coffee that morning. Can I just say I hate
public restrooms; sometimes they are so cold you

can hang meat. Of course there was no hanger for my bags, no lock on the door and worst of all there was no tissue in sight (I was tempted to use the coupon). I told myself it was still better than most missionaries have it. Eventually I made my way back out into the shopping fray. The line to the check-out was even longer but once again I went for it.

I grabbed the item, stood in line again, and finally made it to the cashier. That was when she said, "You'll have to wait just one minute while I clock out and my coworker clocks in." (Oh no, I had been in this store through one entire shift.)

When the new girl was ready I handed her my coupon and the potato masher (there was NO WAY I was letting a 25% off coupon go to waste).

She smiled politely and said, "I'm so sorry, that is not the correct brand of potato masher. Once again she directed my attention to the coupon's fine print. Sure enough I had Brand Y and the coupon was for Brand X (I hadn't even seen those in the back.) "So where do I find Brand X?" I asked trying to keep the vinegar out of my voice.

She smiled a sugary smile, "We sold out of those yesterday."

I walked out of the store and thought to myself "I hope my daughter likes the coupon I got her for Christmas."

Luke 2

We are all pretty familiar with the opening words of Luke 2, *"And it came to pass in those days, that there went out a decree from Caesar Augustus, that all the world should be taxed."* (KJV) Caesar Augustus, a king, worshipped as a god, issued the decree. But he was only a pawn in the hand of The God. So Joseph and Mary made a long trip to Bethlehem even though Mary was *"great with child."*

Did Joseph realize that this was part of the fulfillment from the scripture in Micah 5:2? Did he encourage Mary with that as they traveled? Caesar had wanted to tax the people. Caesar was looking at financial gain and how he could further his own kingdom. But regardless of Caesar's intent, God's plan was still intact. Micah said that the Messiah would be born in Bethlehem.

This is what we can count on, God's Word is truth no matter what the government says. God's Word will be fulfilled exactly the way He wants it. Yes, Caesar was only thinking of his own kingdom, but God was fulfilling His plan for His kingdom.

Day 19

I was mad. It was December and after all I was busy. There were presents to buy and the house to decorate and cookies and candy to make. I always make candy. I had already bought the ingredients, bags of sugar, chocolate chips, nuts, lots of nuts.

Why on earth did this person have to come at Christmas time? But he was coming and since I was the pastor's wife, I was the one to host him while he was in town. Really, a Chinese missionary was coming here to my house at Christmas. I had heard he had come out of China and I knew there would be a story but wasn't there a better time? So okay I would have him, I had resigned myself to it, and besides I had no choice. But I was going to make this simple and not fuss at all. I mean after all Christmas was coming and I needed to be ready for that.

So I prepared for the missionary, minimally, putting my other more important Christmas preparations on hold for the weekend. And then he came. Harry Lee was about my size. He couldn't have been over five foot two and weighed about 120 pounds. He was such a small man. I was struck not only by his stature but also by his quiet demeanor. I offered him some tea.

"Yes, thank you," he said. "But please do not put sugar into it. I want to go back to China and I don't want to be spoiled. There is little sugar in China." I felt a little nudge inside my heart. Spoiled? I had bags of sugar in my pantry and enough chocolate chips to make pounds of fudge. I took him the tea in the living room where he was seated and I sat so I could also listen. My children were already sitting cross-legged on the floor waiting for this interesting looking visitor to share what they hoped was a story.

And he did have a story. He began to tell of his life. "I had been a pastor in Communist China. The leaders had raided my town and taken me as their prisoner. My crime? I had dared to preach about Christ. My punishment was imprisonment. My cell was small enough to touch both walls when standing in the center. I shared this cell with four other men for five years. Every night when I went to sleep we had to sleep side by side. There was not enough room in the cell to sleep otherwise. My place was with my head next to the bucket that was our common toilet.

Our mealtime consisted of one meal a day, one serving of rice. Each day as I left my cell to receive that bowl I would notice the bugs and worms cooked in with the rice and yet I was thankful. I knew though, if I was caught bowing my head there would be retribution. I knew the punishment; it was to hold my hands behind my back and then they were tied. Then they would hang me from my tied hands until the bones in my shoulders were wrenched from their sockets. So as I walked back each day to my tiny cell, instead of bowing, I would lift my eyes toward heaven to thank my Father silently for the food."

I saw his cup was empty. "Would you like some more tea?" I questioned.

"Yes, but please use the same tea bag. I want to go back to China and tea is scarce there. I don't want to be spoiled." He quietly told me.

There it was again, spoiled. How could this quiet, humble man get spoiled from a new tea bag? But I obliged and reused the first one.

He continued and I watched as my children sat transfixed. "I was in that prison for five years. Then one day I was told I was going to be released, not to go home but to go to a different prison, a prison camp. When I got there I could see there were still barriers and guards and cells but there were also fields. My job was to watch over the fields at night so that no one could sneak into the gardens and steal the vegetables in the darkness. I loved being outside after five years in that cell, even if I could not leave by my own choice. Yet I could see the stars at night and I could pray without fear of punishment. For the next seven years this place was my home. Altogether I was imprisoned for twelve years.

For twelve years I was told I could never preach the Gospel again. I was told that it was against the Communist Republic of China to believe my religion, and it was against the law to preach it, telling others about my Savior. I listened to the guards tell me that, and I knew that whenever I had the chance I would tell others about Christ. Finally one day I was released. I had paid for my crime of preaching the Gospel with the last twelve years of my life. Almost as soon as I was released I went to search for my fiancée. I had been engaged to be married when I was taken prisoner. But sometime over the course of those years, when my family and friends knew little about my whereabouts, she had been told that I had died. I heard after my release that she married another man."

I could feel the sadness well up inside me as he spoke of this great pain. For twelve years he had suffered under those men who had beaten him and imprisoned him. For twelve years he had hoped he would see his love again, but then to find out she had married someone else must have been terrible. But as I pondered this I saw his face brighten. "Years have passed," he said. "I had not seen her, but sometime ago a mutual friend told me she is now a widow and after I leave your home I am going to Canada where she now lives with her son. Who knows, maybe for Harry Lee there will yet be great happiness." And he smiled the sweet expression of one in love.

Harry Lee stayed for the whole weekend. Time after time I offered him things. Instead of feeling like it was an imposition, I now felt it was a privilege. Why didn't I get the best meat they had? Why didn't I get better fruit? Why didn't I make those Christmas cookies and candies already so he could have had some and maybe taken some with him? Why was I not better prepared for this sweet, dear saint of God so that he could have had the very best I had to offer?

Why indeed! I knew the answer. It was because I had been selfish and self-centered. Christmas was my time. I loved Christmas and wanted it to be just the way it always was...the way I wanted it. But something had happened. My focus had changed. Harry Lee's presence that weekend had brought my preparations to a screeching halt and yet I received more from his visit than all the Christmas gifts money could buy. I saw the reality of one sold out to a Savior worth suffering for. I saw the life of one who truly lost everything for the cause of Christ and yet joyfully would go back, and I was humbled. If I were called on to face persecution for the cause of Christ, could I? After all, I had not faced inconvenience very well.

Harry Lee did go to Canada and did marry the love of his life. They lived together along with her son for several years. His heart's desire was to go back home, home to China. Harry Lee did go home, but not back to China. Instead a few years ago he went home to meet the One he had preached about and suffered for. The Savior must have greeted him with these words, "Well done good and faithful servant, you have been faithful in a few things, I will make you ruler over much."

His life, his presence in my life was no accident. It was a divine appointment and my life has drastically changed because of it.

Luke 2

Remember Luke 1 was filled with divine appointments. These were lives interrupted with the "suddenlies". In Luke 1, after all his years of serving as an obscure country priest, Zechariah was the one chosen by lot to go into the Temple. He would carry the incense. He would breathe out the prayers for the nation. It came suddenly for Zechariah, but absolutely planned by God. Suddenly his life was moved from obscurity to center stage in God's plan.

Mary was suddenly confronted with her role, carry the child who would carry the sins of the world. Suddenly this divine appointment would carry her from unknown to the most recognized woman who has ever lived. Her life was changed.

Now we see in Luke 2, more divine intervention. All of a sudden, Caesar Augustus just decided to issue a decree which sent everyone packing to their home towns. It just so happened that Joseph was from Bethlehem so they had to go there. It was at the exact time that Mary was due to deliver her Son. And it just so happened that the inn was full. The birth of the Son of God came in a remote little stable, God's divine plan.

Day 20

"She wrapped Him in cloths and placed Him in a manger, because there was no guest room available for them."

A familiar passage at Christmas, there was no room.

Six adult kids, six spouses, seventeen grandchildren, and we all loved to be at home over the holidays. Trouble was not one of us lived in the same state as our Mom. So we journeyed home to northeastern Ohio for Christmas. Southern Indiana, Indianapolis, Chicago, North Carolina, we made our way across dozens of highways, sometimes braved blizzard conditions, drove, walked, rode donkeys, so we could be home.

Six kids, six spouses and seventeen grandchildren, it was a challenge for even our very creative mom to coordinate sleeping arrangements. The house was big enough for a widowed, fifty-something mom, even large by some standards, but Christmas was an invasion. Now the children were easy enough. Mom took every quilt known to man and laid them on the floor of the living room and that was the children's bedroom. If you ask them today for a Christmas memory, cousins camping out in front of the Christmas tree is an all-time favorite. The brightly lit Christmas tree sparkled away, and seventeen little heads bobbed up and down, giggling, laughing, until dads would threaten retribution for "One more sound!"

But the adults, now that was a different story. We've all heard the adage, "Location, location, location!" That was true at Mom's. There was the prime realty, the bedroom in the finished basement. It was dark, away from much of the noise and the couple who slept there actually enjoyed the best sleep. There were two other bedrooms that were on the main floor that also offered quiet repose and rest. Mom gave up her bed for the couch, so sweet, so gracious, but our widowed mother owned twin beds. Need I say more? Then there was the pull-out bed in the basement family room. The problem there was you could not go to bed until everyone else had called it quits for the night. And then, as soon as anyone got up, you were also up. But that site was still better than the location that in most circles would be termed a fixer-upper, a place that needed a little TLC. I'm speaking of course of that seldom used bedroom space under the dining room table in front of the freezing sliding glass doors.

Ah yes, location, location, location. This is how it worked. The first to arrive at Mom's got to choose where they wanted to sleep. Five minutes could make all the difference in the entire Christmas experience. The last to arrive, well, Linda still speaks of the scars she carries by being awakened in the night by a bright, blinding light. No, not angels, this was the light reflecting off of the white legs of one of the brothers-in-law in his mighty short Karate robe as he opened the refrigerator for a 2:00 AM snack. She could identify with the terrified shepherds, but no comforting words of "Don't be afraid, I bring you good news", just a mumbled, "Sorry!"

Luke 2

Luke 2:6-7 When Mary and Joseph arrived in Bethlehem, the best rooms were already full. The worst rooms were already taken. The only accommodation left was the least accommodating. It was a barn, a stable, a place for animals. When my children were born I wanted clean, pristine. I wanted the scent of antiseptic. For Mary it was dirt and smells and unpleasantness.

Why would the God of the Universe allow His pure, clean Son to be born in a place for sheep and goats and beasts of burden? We are not told for sure, but we do know that Jesus is the Lamb of God.

He is the One who would bear our burdens. And perhaps God wanted us to know that if His pure, clean, radiant, righteous Son could be born in this dirty, unclean place, He could be born in our dirty, unclean hearts.

Day 21

Gifts. I have to admit that I have had my fair share and many of them I don't even remember. If you were to ask me to list all I received last Christmas, I would probably have a hard time.

But there are gifts that I have no trouble recalling. I remember sitting at the foot of the Rocky Mountains on a morning that was so cold you could see your breath, even though it was mid-June. First one up, I was outside of our little cabin, with a steaming cup of coffee in my hand. It was a brand new, stoneware mug imprinted with a moose. My Bible was in my other hand.

My husband had just given me a beautiful, brown, evergreen and rust wool blanket. We found it in a little shop in Montana. One side was a soft plush pile. The other had the sturdiness of an old army blanket. I wrapped myself in its folds and propped my feet on the picnic table bench. I felt the kiss of the cold on my face but the warmth of the blanket around me. It couldn't have been a more perfect parable to me as I looked up at the mountains and saw the awesome majesty of the Lord. I was reminded of the things that sometimes sting me but the arms of the Good Shepherd that hold me close and shield me from cold realities.

I have been back to that little shop in Montana several times but have never found another blanket like it. The blanket is on the back of my couch in my living room and I have to tell you, it is one of my favorite things. It is beautiful and my sisters would all love it on the back of their couches. But it isn't just the blanket. It is the lesson.

Now isn't that a fun way to learn!

Luke 2

As night settled in, most of Bethlehem settled down, but not Mary. The hardest work of her young life began. She was laboring to bring her child into the world. The Bible gives us little information about the birth. It simply says in Luke 2:7 *"and she gave birth to her firstborn, a son. She wrapped him in cloths and placed Him in a manger, because there was no guest room available for them."* We read it; she lived it.

While childbirth is very natural, it is also intensely painful and difficult. Joseph was the only one to assist her. Did he cry out to God on her behalf as she cried out in pain? Did he wipe her forehead and kiss her cheek as her labor grew more intense?

Finally the pain and travail were over. Mary's son was born. She didn't have a beautiful wool blanket, only strips of cloth. She didn't have a perfect cradle, only a feeding trough. But with joy more intense than the pain, she looked into the face of her child. All who have given birth can identify with her. But Mary looked not only at the face of her son, she looked into the face of God's Son.

Gabriel had told her the Lord was with her. Perhaps in that moment she knew beyond a shadow of a doubt, because she cradled Him, The God of the Universe, in her arms.

Day 22

OK, here I am again. You're probably tired of my cooking stories. You probably think cooking is all I do. Are you kidding? Think about that...

It's part of the reason I'm such a failure at it. But it is the reason that I buy a lot of barbecue sauce. You should try it on cake sometime!

My daughter came home from school one day and said she needed to take a cake for a party. I said, "Ok sure, what kind of cake do you want?" Her response was, "Do you think we could call Aunt Karen?" My feelings were hurt.

When we asked our son to thank the Lord for the food, he would always slip in a plea that it would be good. I have to wonder what impact that had on his faith. He came home one day when I was making tuna casserole and asked, "Mom, are we having company?"

"Why do you ask?"

"Because you don't usually cook this good just for us."

One day he asked if I could make the crunchy stuff he had eaten at Aunt Kathie's house. Growing up in our home he hadn't learned what to call it. I finally figured out he was asking for bacon. My breakfast expertise was limited to fixing cold cereal.

It wasn't long ago that my husband returned from a church camp and we were going to eat together for the first time in about a week.

I had fixed a great meal, had it all ready, but he had to wash the vans, get a service guy to work on the bus, make sure that every kid got home with the right parent. (It makes promoting the next event a little easier when you do that successfully.) But of course that made him late.

Someone once asked if running late counts as exercise. My husband should be a walking skeleton. When he finally got home, I apologized with the words, "I'm sorry, but I cooked the life out of the chicken." As I think about that, it really was an accomplishment since the chicken was dead to begin with.

Half a bottle of barbecue sauce later, I apologized again. "No," he said. "I like chicken jerky!"
The next day we were grocery shopping together. I ran to pick up a few things while he picked up stuff for a church event. When I returned, there was a very large bag sitting in the cart that I couldn't identify. I picked it up and he started laughing. "It's chicken jerky!"

He must have liked supper. (Maybe I had accidentally stumbled onto a great recipe.)

I read the package and then said, "I'm going to put this back. Where did you get it?"

He said "Why? I like chicken jerky."

I looked at him and smiled, "BECAUSE THESE ARE DOG TREATS!"

Ruined again!

Failure proof breakfast recipes from my house to yours

Recipe 1
1 cup of circular shaped oat cereal
Add milk
Serve immediately

Recipe 2
1 cup granola
Add skim milk to taste
Serve immediately

Recipe 3
Crunchy stuff (I've learned this...do not boil, call my sister for bacon recipe)
Have her serve immediately

Recipe 4
Christmas Breakfast
Chocolate chip cookie cereal
Add red and green sprinkles
Cover with chocolate milk
Serve immediately
Enjoy

Luke 2

Luke 2:7 says *"and she brought forth her first born son, wrapped Him in swaddling clothes and laid Him in a manger..."* (KJV)

It was no accident that Jesus was laid in a manger, a feeding trough. During His ministry He would say, *"Very truly I tell you, unless you eat the flesh of the Son of Man and drink his blood, you have no life in you."* John 6:53

It was no accident that Jesus, The Bread of Life, was born in Bethlehem. Bethlehem means the House of Bread.

It was no accident that Jesus, The Lamb of God, was born in a stable, and that shepherds came to attend this Lamb.

It was no accident that Jesus was wrapped in swaddling clothes.

Making chicken jerky? Yes, that was an accident. But NOTHING about the birth of Christ was an accident. It was all a MIRACLE just for us.

Day 23

I teach kindergarten. I often say that they won't promote me because my math skills don't reach beyond addition facts to five. Once in a while I even catch myself counting on my fingers. But I do hope my students like school. I did have one of them tell me the other day that he wished he could live at school because he loves it so much. I am delighted that we are kicking off his school career on such a positive note. But we all know that we can't live at school.

However, I almost do. I was there a little after 5:00 AM yesterday. They've given me the code because I'm usually the first one in the building. I left there after 5:00 PM. Believe me, it can't be that I am that thorough. I think it's because I'm that scatter brained. I try so hard to stay organized so I find a place for everything and put everything in its place. But then I have to go on a massive hunt to find it because I can't remember my organization process.

It's not like I put my keys in the freezer or store my purse in the mailbox, I have things a little better under control than that. I've never misplaced a student or gotten on the wrong bus for a field trip, so it is safe for you to enroll your child in my class. But for the little things like remembering where I put the science movie or what closet I put the brightly

colored, fruit flavored cereal for the pattern neck-
laces, I often have to look. I spend a lot more time
searching than I do finding.

It would help if I could leave myself some clues. It's
good that I like unravelling mysteries because I get
to do it so often.

Luke 2

But let's leave my classroom for now and step onto the Bethlehem hillside. We're going to take a deep breath, and join the shepherds for a few days as we look at some of the clues and begin to unravel a little of the mystery.

At first glance it seems unlikely that a band of shepherds with leather like skin, dirt under their nails, feet smelly from tramping through sheep dung, should be the first to witness the birth of the Savior of the world. But if you look at it a little closer it makes all the sense of eternity.

They were given some very specific clues so we can see why they were very specifically chosen.

The angel said that the baby had been born in the town of David. The shepherds understood that right away. These shepherds lived outside the city limits. David had been a shepherd just like them. He too had cared for his sheep on those same hills. Every day they put their feet right where he had walked. They knew David had become a king. They were going to find THE King.

This little place was named Bethlehem. It means "House of Bread". The One to come was to be the Bread of Life.

He would be wrapped in strips of cloth. These shepherds were probably very familiar with what that meant. Many of the sheep raised outside of Bethlehem were to become the lambs sacrificed at the Temple on Passover. If a lamb had that destiny, it had to be perfect. These shepherds would sometimes wrap the wobbly legs of a newborn lamb in strips of cloth to protect it. They were experts on recognizing perfect lambs. Who better to go to search for the Perfect Lamb of God?

This baby would be lying in a manger. These shepherds would have known every spot where one of those was stationed. It is most likely that this baby would have been the only one in all of Bethlehem that was nestled in a feeding trough for the night. And then of course, there was the the chorus of angels that interrupted the quiet nighttime sky with an announcement that is still echoing today. The light from those dazzling heralds would have filled the eyes of those shepherds and flooded their souls.

There had probably been times as they sat outside of Jerusalem, that they had front row seats to a spectacular light show when giant lamp stands outside of the Temple would have been lit to cast their light throughout the region. What is incredibly significant about that is that those giant lamp stands were filled with oil and ignited with an unusual wick. It was a tightly wrapped cord of cloth made from the worn out garments of the Temple priests. The strips of cloth were called swaddling clothes. The shepherds were going to find the Light of the World.

They hurried off and found Him.

And when they did they realized that the clues were only a hint. What these dirty, smelly shepherds got to experience was the reality of worshipping Heavenly Royalty.

They had found Him.

Luke 2:16 says that *"they had hurried off and found Mary and Joseph, and the baby, who was lying in the manger."*

He wants us to find Him too, not because He is lost but because we are. There are so many clues that He is the Bread of Life, the Lamb of God, the Light of the World. We challenge you to look for them. When you do, you also will experience the reality of worshiping Heavenly Royalty.

Day 24

For some reason I have terrible discerning skills when it comes to public restrooms.

To sum it up, I get it wrong. I teach reading so I think I can read the signs. I recognize the skirt on the icon for the women's bathroom. I can even tell you that the cute names like "cowgirls" and "cowboys" or "chickens" and "roosters" indicate that one is for women and one is for men. You can check for yourself that there are any number of "interesting" names for public restrooms and I honestly do have the mental capacity to figure them out.

But I still get it wrong.

I have bad cooking stories and bad bathroom stories. As you read through this little book, all of those are my experiences. It speaks volumes about me. And none of it is good.

One of my most humiliating bathroom encounters took place on a mission trip to Wisconsin.

We were traveling with a large group of teenagers and adults to a Native American camp. Most of us recognized each other. We even knew most everyone's name. What we didn't know was that the task ahead of us would be mammoth. As soon as we left the vans and stepped onto camp soil, we would have to be on mission. Reaching those children with the Gospel was a job that was too big for us to do. But may I interject a brief side note. Many times God's tasks are bigger than we are. He does it on purpose so we have to depend on Him. Don't get nervous when you think the task is too big. Get nervous when you think the task is too small.

When you travel with a huge group of people it means that bathroom breaks are frequent and long. So we combined this one with lunch at a couple of fast food restaurants. The kids all headed for the food. I headed for the bathroom. I thought I was the only one to structure my priorities in this way. I ran into the stall and then came out quickly to wash my hands. One of the men from our trip was standing in MY bathroom. Horrified, I announced, "You're in the wrong bathroom!"

He responded much more calmly than I had. "No, I'm not."

Suddenly the whole picture came into focus. He was standing in front of a piece of equipment that doesn't exist in women's bathrooms. When he had spoken to me he had only turned his head and given me the word that I was actually the one who was in the wrong place.

And then I realized why he was standing with his back to me.

I could almost not breathe. Hysterical blindness was well within my reach. I ran out the door. I looked for my husband. I had to tell someone who could pat me on the shoulder and tell me it was okay. I am a pastor's wife, fairly insecure, and pretty determined to live in such a way that others can follow my example. Being in the wrong bathroom with a man DID NOT FIT THAT PROFILE AT ALL.

My husband had taken the vans to get them filled up with gas. He was nowhere around. I hunted down one of my sisters. I had to get a perspective on this. As soon as I saw her, I blurted out the whole story in a breathless whisper. I was searching her face for some indication as to how big a mistake she thought I had just made. Instead she looked at me sympathetically and simply said, "I know."

I was dumbfounded. "What do you mean that you know? How can you know?"

Her response was too calm. "One of the guys told us."

"Us?" What did that mean? "Does everyone know?" She shook her head. "No, there's a Japanese couple in the restaurant. I'm pretty sure they don't speak English. I don't think they know."

I was ruined.

We still had hours on the road until we reached the camp. And I have to tell you, no one wanted to let this go. The teasing went on and on. It had finally died down a little when the guy that had shared the bathroom encounter with me shouted out, "Could we stop at the next restroom? I have to use the Little Girl's Room."

And it began again.

I have to be honest with you. I was horribly embarrassed. I wanted the teasing to stop. It didn't. So I prayed about it.

Now I don't want you to get the wrong idea about me. I'm not super spiritual. I am not a bit mystical. But there have been sometimes in my life that I have known that the Lord was speaking to me and this was one of them.

Most of the time, when He speaks to me like that, He whispers. I have to listen.

This is what He said, "Kris, you are the bonding tool."

So what did that mean? It meant that the jokes, the laughter, the teasing were putting everyone on the same page. They got to know each other as they laughed. Walls broke down. Those who felt a little out of sync got pulled into the group. Those, who felt a little inferior, saw that they were a step above me.

It worked. By the time we reached Crandon, Wisconsin, we weren't just a collection of individuals, we were a team. It was what the task required. God can bind a team anyway He chooses. This time it was over a bathroom mistake.

Sometimes the most amazing results come out of the most humbling and even humiliating circumstances. I think there were about twenty-five kids who came to know Christ on that trip.

I only had the privilege of a tiny part of that victory. Was it worth it? I would say a resounding "Yes!" But I think in eternity my response will be even louder.

Luke 2

Let's take a moment to talk about some very over-used words. "I'm bored. I am just so bored!"

Hmmm, boredom? In our high tech culture, how can that be? How many channels do we have on the TV? How many games can we play on our phones? How many toys do we have either in the garage or in the playroom? How many interesting places can our fingertips take us on the computer? How many breathtaking destinations can we visit on a vacation? Books, magazines, restaurants, music, movies, sporting events...sure, in our world we think we have every right to say, "We are bored".

But most often boredom does not come because we have too little. It comes because we have too much. We are standing in line waiting for life in the amusement park. Where is the next big ride and how long do I have to wait? The thrills have to get larger and the gaps between have to get smaller. The immediate becomes the goal. I want it big and I want it now. But when all the thrills are gone for the day and we think we stand before an empty horizon, we dare to proclaim our boredom. The anticipation, looking forward, has been dropped to the floor, swept under an old rug and replaced with a "must have" in the now. It doesn't matter if I can't afford it. It doesn't matter if it belongs to someone else. It doesn't matter if it isn't exactly what I thought I wanted. I want it now because I am bored.

Okay, so let's talk about what could have been real boredom. Sitting in the late afternoon sun, on the dusty brown Bethlehem hillside, there is almost nothing more boring than watching sheep graze. Unless of course it would be several hours later on that same Bethlehem hillside under the darkened evening sky, watching sheep sleep.

But were they bored? We have no way of knowing. Did they sigh over listening to the many hours of silence? Did they hate sitting on a dusty hillside or meandering the unhurried pace of a flock of sheep? Was the big thrill of most days spotting the watering trough? Occasionally there would have been the adrenaline rush of the chase when a bear or mountain lion dared to enter the fields. But was it enough to drive away the tedium? We don't know. But we do know this, their lives were about to be interrupted with a bigness that is beyond description. They were about to go on mission and mission erases boredom.

That night the shepherds were minding their own business, just doing what they had done a thousand times before. Suddenly the night sky was lit up by the Shekinah, God's Glory. In Luke 2:10 the angel said to them, *"Do not be afraid. I bring you good news that will cause great joy for all the people."* This was a spiritual encounter and spiritual encounters are never boring.

Day 25

I went to visit my family in another city. My mother, sister, daughter and her husband all attend the same church. My sister was out of town but my son-in-law was speaking at church. I was there to hear him. I look enough like my sister that people instantly recognize the relationship. In fact our hair is very similar in length, style and color. So I was standing at the back of the church next to our mother (this helped identify who I am) with the under-the-balcony seats behind me. Suddenly I felt an arm around me. A woman I had seen at the church, but did not truly know, was hugging me. "Hi, you are the sister." She sweetly said. "I knew you couldn't BE your sister because she is half your size."

HALF YOUR SIZE! (Someone told me long ago that when you write in all capitals it is like shouting, so let me say that again) HALF YOUR SIZE! Now isn't that a special Christmas gift! Those are just the words you long to hear before the worship service begins. I swallowed a couple of times and tried to smile back. I managed to say, "Yes, she has become the goal. I want to look just like her."

I joined the same weight tracking site that she did. She has actually lost pounds and mine has crawled down in ounces. We get updates. Today hers says that she lost 1.7 pounds since her last weigh in (which, by the way, was yesterday). Mine says nothing because I refuse to log it until it goes down again and who knows when that will be. It has stayed the same for weeks.

We even went on vacation together but we carefully logged the calories. We ate the SAME thing. I watched. If anything she had a few more calories because her coffee had sugar. Mine did not. When we got back her weight was down...mine was up a bit. UGHHHH.

Maybe you struggle with some of these same issues. Maybe you look in the mirror and wish you could look like someone else. Maybe others have said words that hurt. So what are we going to believe? People look at the outside and here's the thing, whenever we compare ourselves to others we can get in trouble. We can either say, "I'm no good because that person is so much better than me" Or we say. "I'm really great because I am so much better than he or she." And when it gets right down to it, neither one of those is correct.

God looks at the heart and this is what He says, "You are fearfully and wonderfully made." So now did you get that? FEARFULLY and WONDER-FULLY made. It means we are made in His image. We have been designed especially for His kingdom. So I have a job to do that only I can do. Now maybe that's a little scary, a job that only I can do for the Kingdom of God.

Here is what I love, most of the time in Scripture the ones God called were the unlikely ones. They were not the most beautiful, the wealthiest, the most educated, the most put-together, the skinniest, (I added that for my own self esteem). They were often the ones who, by any other standard, were those who could not do the job. That means that God had to do it through them.

So yes, He made me for a purpose, with my imperfections, my weight troubles, my insecurities, even my talents or lack of talents, God can use me, just like He chose to use Mary. Of course her job was big; she was carrying Jesus, the Son of God, the Savior of the World. But once we accept Christ as our Savior we carry Him too and our job is to take Him to a world full of people with insecurities, imperfections, talents and lack of talents.

Luke 2

Luke 2:8-20. One of my favorite themes in the book of Luke is...those who cannot are the very ones who do. So let's recap.

Most likely Luke was a Gentile, not an apostle. Who would have thought he could be one of the Gospel writers, and yet...

Elizabeth and Zechariah were old, too old to have a child. Elizabeth was barren, and yet...

Mary was a virgin. She couldn't possibly have a child, and yet...

Shepherds at this time were considered unclean, because of their dealing with animals. They were viewed as thieves, only a cut above lepers and were not allowed to give testimony in a court of law, and yet...

It was out there on Bethlehem's hillside that the God of the Universe chose those shepherds to be the first witnesses of His Son's birth, and to be the very ones to share the testimony and spread the word.

Our God is not limited by what we think is possible because there is always...and yet...

Day 26

I'm a little like my brown house. Part of the brown comes from the hair color that my beautician whips up. It's my natural color; it just comes from a bottle. I have a growing tan that someone has very rudely termed "age spots." My wrinkles are not only in my carpet, they are on my face. Yes, I'm a little like my brown house.

I am an unspectacular person. Ordinary is a pretty good word used to describe me.

Most of the time shadows are better seen than I am. For example, once my husband and our youth intern (who is also my nephew) were visiting the hospital. This young man had fairly long, curly hair and was about my husband's size. Now, we do share the same first name. His name is C-H-R-I-S and mine is K-R-I-S. But that is where the resemblance ends. He's the one who says that he has a big brain and I have a little brain. But I say he could double for Sasquatch (definition: a large, hairy, humanoid creature said to live in wilderness areas) and I think I could double for NOT Sasquatch (definition: still ordinary but better looking than a large, hairy, humanoid creature said to live in wilderness areas).

But with that being said, remember my husband and Chris were visiting with a lady in the hospital. They talked with her, and prayed with her.

Then as they were about to leave, she said, "Now, tell me your wife's name again."

Did you get that? She thought my nephew was me! Talk about being unspectacular!

I want you to understand. I am okay with being unspectacular. Many of the people of the Book were.

Luke 2

Think about the shepherds from Luke 2:8-20 and once again walk back to the fields with me. There was nothing remarkable about that evening. The sheep didn't bleat to the tune of Silent Night. The stars didn't twinkle in the colors of Christmas. This was an ordinary night in an ordinary field. These were unspectacular shepherds living life in the shadows.

But their lives were about to be interrupted with a *"suddenly!"* There they were, watching their sheep graze when *"an angel of the Lord appeared to them and the glory of the Lord shown around them." And then "Suddenly, a great company of the heavenly host appeared with the angel, praising God and saying, 'Glory to God in the highest heaven, and on earth peace to those on whom His favor rests.'"*

And they were given a message and a mission. They went to see and they left to tell.

The unremarkable, the unspectacular, became part of the miraculous. It happened *"suddenly."*

Christmas is a time for just such moments. Actually every day is.

I am not spectacular. I am not remarkable. I am a little like my brown house. But I can be a part of a "suddenly." It can happen as I read His Word. It can happen as I listen to a message or a worship song. It can absolutely happen as I join the mission and share the message. It can happen as I walk into a Christmas worship experience. I can go to see but I can leave to tell.

The unremarkable becomes the remarkable. The ordinary becomes the extraordinary. The unspectacular becomes the spectacular. It happens *"suddenly."*

Day 27

It was December 24th. The checklist for our Christmas Eve and Christmas Day celebrations began in my head. The chicken soup for our traditional Christmas Eve supper was simmering happily away in my crock pot. The perfectly lovely thing about soup is that it's pretty hard to dry it out.

I had already picked up the doughnuts for the Christmas breakfast, lots of doughnuts, cream-filled, chocolate covered long johns, big fruit fritters dunked in glaze, chocolate cake donuts with chocolate icing and sprinkles, and so on. Everyone's favorite. The coffee pots were set up and ready to turn on. The potatoes were boiled and peeled for the morning's fried potatoes. Sausage had already been grilled and waited in a foil package in the freezer, ready to pull out and pop in the oven in the morning. I had eggs; I had bacon, (I'm one of the sisters who actually knows how to make the crunchy stuff), even a little left-over steak from another Christmas get-together. Yum, breakfast would be perfect. The gifts were all bought, no last minute frantic purchases this year. They were beautifully wrapped and under the tree. Mentally the check list checked out. I had everything done, everything ready. It would be perfect. Ah yes... PERFECT.

This was one of those rare days when everything that could be done, was done. And now, it was a day to play. The out-of-town sister was in town and we were about to head out for a little Dec. 24th shopping. What a perfect way to spend a few golden hours before all the family get-togethers. The bargains on Christmas decorations could have already begun. Who knew? We just might find that perfect deal of the century. After a bath and dressing I had that sister on the phone. While we were arranging our excursion, I came downstairs.

Suddenly all I could do was yell, "Oh no! OH! NO!!"

"What's wrong?" My sister screamed back.

It was raining, noooo, water was pouring down from the ceiling. All the bath water from my six foot tub was somehow drenching my family room, onto my wood floors, covering my furniture, showering my Christmas tree and destroying my perfectly wrapped gifts. I could hardly form the words to tell my sister. I couldn't grab towels fast enough. I yelled for my husband. He grabbed towels and the phone to call a plumber. What would that cost on Christmas Eve?

Ah, the best laid plans... My perfect day to play had just become a day to work, redo, tear down, clean up, wash up, dry off, put away. My perfect Christmas tree, now perfectly soaked, was undecorated, taken down, boxed up, and placed on a shelf in the garage. The gifts were set aside to, hopefully, dry out. My illusions of perfection were wrung out and literally went down the drain.

But, even as I scrubbed and cleaned and washed and dried, I kept telling myself, "It's just a house, just a wood floor, leather furniture, just a tree, nothing is wet that can't be dried out or cleaned up, or set aside until next year. Our children are well, the grandchildren perfect. God still loves us and sent His Son for us."

Suddenly, unexpected gratitude flooded my heart as I cleaned up my flooded house. Perhaps that first Christmas didn't quite go the way Mary had thought either. Ah yes! As it turned out it really was... A PERFECT CHRISTMAS.

Luke 2

The perfect Christmas...we strive for perfection. We look for the right gifts, just the right thing for all the special people on our list. We cook and bake and clean and decorate and set up and put up and wrap up all the things we think of as constituting a perfect Christmas.

Let's look back at that first Christmas:
Mary was unmarried and pregnant, a death sentence in ancient Nazareth. (Luke 1)

Joseph was ready to divorce her. Evidently he didn't believe that she was telling him the truth when she told him that this was of God. Obviously he still loved her because he wanted to do it privately, to keep her indiscretion and pregnancy a secret, but he was not willing to marry a girl of her now tarnished reputation. It took an angelic visitor to convince him. (Matthew 1)

Mary was in her ninth month of pregnancy when she and Joseph discovered that they would have to travel to Bethlehem to register for a tax, about a ninety mile walk on a good day. (Luke 2)

No room, no privacy, no cleanliness, no midwife or doctor, no experienced older woman to walk her down this path, no soft clean sheets for her, no warm blankets for the baby, no bed for her son, no soft gentle music, just the mooing of cattle and the baa's of the sheep. (Luke 2)

Nothing perfect except...Jesus, God with us, Immanuel, Savior, Redeemer, Bread of Life, Light of the World, Lamb of God, King of Kings, Lord of Lords, Creator, Sustainer, Friend. (Matthew, Mark, Luke, John and all the rest of the Scripture).

Absolutely and unequivocally, a perfect Christmas.

Day 28

Christmas is supposed to be a joyful time, and for many, maybe even for most, it is. But not for all. Sometimes painful things, very painful things, happen at Christmas. And so it was for me. I was home alone when there was a knock on my door. The man standing there had a look on his face. You have to understand, it was not the first time someone had approached me with that same look. It is a look that says "I have something I must tell you, but it hurts me greatly to do so". This man was pained because he had seen my husband.

Infidelity is a very ugly word. It is one of those words that makes you hurt to think it, saying it brings it to a more dreadful level. But living it is so much more devastating. When the one you thought you could trust, the one you committed to, is committed to someone else, the pain reaches epic levels. Separation followed and on Christmas he was with her. I spent much of that Christmas in the fetal position. I was crushed, broken, and just like so much trash left on the side of the road, I felt like I had been thrown away. My dear family kept telling me to rest, take a deep breath, try to stay calm.

But through the pain of that, something beautiful emerged. The One who is always faithful, the One who never lies, the One who never forsakes, lifted my head. It didn't happen in a day, or a month, or even right away that year, but it did happen.

Little by little, the disgrace, the shame, the pain flowed out of me and God replaced it with His sweet presence. That Christmas and many days after that I slept with my Bible right next to me. I grew to be so dependent on what He had to say, and my heart healed. Peace and forgiveness have replaced sadness and devastation.

In Luke 2 it says that *"Mary treasured up all of these things and pondered them in her heart"*. I can identify with that verse. Although there was pain there was also the treasure of God's Word and over the years, I have looked back over things and pondered. Sometimes I have even asked God "Why?".

But at this point I know that I don't have to know why. It's because I know WHO. It is through Him, the One who knew suffering for me, that no matter what I face, He brings me through it.

Luke 2

The Bible records in Luke 2:19 that *"Mary treasured up all these things and pondered them in her heart"*.

The visit from Gabriel, the trip to see Elizabeth, the confirmation from Elizabeth that she was carrying the son of God, Joseph's reaction and his dream, the long journey to Bethlehem, the stable, and now the shepherds telling her that an angel had said to come...so many things to hold onto. There were so many things she wanted to remember about this. Each one was a miracle and she looked at each miracle as a treasure and hid them away in her heart. I have things to remember as well.

God's Word is filled with miracles and these are the treasures that I want to ponder and hide in my heart.

Day 29

There is one more part to my sixth grade saga. For a moment my brother and I stood, transfixed, frozen on the stairway to the basement, not really believing our eyes. The hope of a bicycle was no longer a mere hope. It was a reality. There it stood, a real life flesh and blood bicycle...well okay, steel and fine plastic. But there it stood. There might have been a moment of hesitation...should I go down to touch it, to ride it, to feel its cold steel under my feet.

But in reality all I could think about was the opportunity to share this great good news. My siblings were upstairs suffering with their own disappointment, fighting back their own tears, believing that this Christmas was sparse. They had also wanted and waited and hoped. But I now knew there was more to this Christmas than gloves, games and pajamas. This was the biggest Christmas we had ever had. I ran. I jumped. I leaped. I think I flew. It was my privilege. It was my joy to scream out the words, "THERE ARE BIKES IN THE BASEMENT! COME AND SEE! WE GOT BIKES!"

Christmas day was transformed from dire to delight. This was life changing. We got bikes and we were going to ride them. It didn't matter to us that there was snow. It didn't matter that there were huge drifts. Did we wear coats? I think we may not have even put on shoes. I know we still had on pajamas. We didn't care. We had bikes.

In a few short years I would come to realize that even this Christmas, with the gift of a glorious new bicycle, was not big enough. My view was too narrow, too small. It is now my privilege, my joy to share this great good news, "WE HAVE A SAVIOR!"

While the gift of receiving Christ is life changing, it is even bigger. It is world changing. It is eternity changing.

Luke 2

"The shepherds returned, glorifying and praising God for all the things they had heard and seen, which were just as they had been told." Luke 2:20.

The shepherds had seen the miraculous, the awesome, the face of God. It was so easy to be filled with praise and worship. But I get to experience the miraculous as well. It is in the pages of Scripture.

It is there that God's face is revealed. It is there I can see that things are happening in my world today just as they had been foretold, and I am filled with praise.

Day 30

For so many years of my life, at 11:00 PM on Christmas Eve, I knew exactly where I would be. It was at a little country church in Robertsville, Ohio.

There was music, singing, and of course candles. It was, after all, a candlelight service. We had a live nativity, most often the children were dressed in bathrobes, homemade costumes, and tinsel halos. The Pastor kept the message short, because it was, after all, nearly midnight. The lights were dimmed and the candles lit. Funny thing about candlelight, it begins with one little light that is shared, but sharing light doesn't diminish it. Sharing a candy bar, or a piece of pie, you only get half. Sharing light you get double, and quadruple, and on and on until the light fills the place. In that little country church, only the glow from the candles and the light from the tree illuminated the sanctuary. Yet it was filled with light. It was beautiful, memorable, Christmas light at its best.

At midnight we blew out our candles and walked out into the cold night air of northeastern Ohio. Often snow would be gently falling and I knew that Christmas had come. It was a quiet beauty, a reverent moment, a small taste of the awe of that first Christmas night.

Luke 2

On that first Christmas Eve, all those years ago, the shepherds saw the light. They also heard a message. It wasn't a very long message for them either; it was, after all, the middle of the night. Luke 2:8-20 tells us what they heard, *"Today in the town of David a Savior has been born to you; He is the Messiah, the Lord. This will be a sign to you: you will find a baby wrapped in cloths and lying in a manger."*

They couldn't wait, they had to go and see for themselves and sure enough, they found Mary and Joseph and Jesus, the Light of the world. When they had seen Him, they spread the word concerning what they had been told, what they had witnessed with their own eyes.

Funny thing about sharing good news, it doesn't diminish it, it only grows, not just in the number of people who hear, but in our hearts as well. We have the same opportunity as the shepherds did to go and spread the Word, share the Light, tell the Good News and let it grow and grow until it fills the world.

Day 31

Luke 2:19 *"But Mary treasured up all these things and pondered them in her heart."* Mary took these special moments and tucked them away so she could bring them out and look at them from time to time, perhaps a difficult time in the future when the sweetness of these snapshots would help sustain her. Let me tell you about one of those moments I keep tucked away in my heart.

We were not the likely candidates for adoption. My husband and I already had three biological daughters, but for some unknown reason God began to work in our hearts to adopt a baby boy. We expected closed doors. We expected to be told "No!" But when God wants a door open, it opens. The day came when a beautiful red-headed six month old baby boy joined our family. That first night we kissed him good night, laid him in his crib, and you know what? He slept through the night. My husband said, "We should have gotten all our kids at six months."

That first Sunday we took him to church and wanted him dedicated, just as Mary and Joseph took Jesus to the Temple for his dedication. My husband and I were at the back of the church waiting for the end of the service.

I said to my sister, "Where are the girls?"

Kris said, "Karen, don't worry about it."

I looked up front and realized my daughters were on the stage looking like they were ready to sing. They had sung together at church only one other time. It was a song that began something like this: "We are not descended from monkeys though you may be fooled at first glance..." I remember thinking that the song was not really appropriate for their new little brother's baby dedication.

But then out of my sweet little girls' mouths came these words, "Welcome to the family. We're glad that you have come to share your life with us..." One of my dear friends, Kathy, had taught that song to them unbeknown to my husband or to me.

My husband began to weep. The little girls began to cry. I was nearly doubled over with weeping. The Pastor was wiping tears. My brother-in-law, who is one of the other Pastors, couldn't speak. I'm not sure there was a dry eye in the place. Our son even showed his delight by spitting up all over my husband's suit. The effort my friend put into teaching the girls the song was a gift. This sweet surprise, kept by my daughters, was a gift. The moment of pure joy, holding our new son, and having him be so welcomed, well it was, purely and simply, a gift that I have so treasured in my heart.

Luke 2

In Luke 2:22, Mary and Joseph took Jesus to the Temple in Jerusalem to be dedicated. A man named Simeon had been waiting there for the Messiah. When he saw Jesus, he knew the wait was finally over. Jesus was the promised One.

I wonder if Simeon had gone every day with the expectation that today might be the day that He would get to see God's promise revealed. Because Simeon was looking, he saw. When I come to Scripture, do I come with that same sense of anticipation, of expectation, that I will get to see God's promises revealed? Jesus is standing in the shadow of every page.

O Lord God, give me eyes that I may see. Help me to look so I can know...You.

Day 32

I have met the Ghost of Christmas Past. Oh, he didn't show up exactly at the stroke of midnight on a cold Christmas Eve, but he was as frightening as old Marley in the door knocker and as confining as the unseen chains around Scrooge.

He goes by numerous names. We have all heard them. Regret, Bitterness, Selfishness, Guilt, Hurt. There are many more but you probably recognize him too, even though he may have visited you under a different name.

He wears a death kerchief tied around his skeletal face and speaks in a haunting tone. He arrives to make me remember...not the pleasant, bring-a-smile to your face memories, but those that hurt. We have asked you to join us on the wings of some of our most joyful memories. We have held hands skipping down a lane named Laughter. We have asked you to sit in the shade of our Victory Garden. But what do you do with the ghost of Christmas Past? What do you do when your memories don't bring you happiness, but bring you tears? I am not talking about healing tears. I am talking about bitter tears that leave trails down your face and scars down your heart.

This ghost is an enemy and we need a weapon against him.

He came to visit because old Scrooge sat in a cold, dark room that reflected his cold, dark heart. He took gold and silver coins and hugged them around him thinking they could bring him warmth.
They didn't. They were as icy as steel.

He thought ignoring the day would make it all go away. It didn't.

 It won't for us either.

What most people don't know is that Scrooge would not have had to wait for three ghosts to visit him on that fateful Christmas Eve in order to do an about face in his life. He actually carried the answer with him.

His name is Ebenezer. It is a Hebrew word. It is used in the Bible in 1 Samuel 7:12. It means "foundation stone" or "The Lord has helped us."

I understand that the story, *The Christmas Carol*, is fiction and Charles Dickens could write the redemption of his leading character any way he wanted.

But we can't.

There is only one way of redemption and that is a Christmas gift that is beyond any other.

The angel told the shepherds that he had come to bring them good news of great joy. The Savior had been born that night but that Savior was never intended to stay in a manger cradle. It is where many people like to leave Him. But the news of His birth was just the beginning to the story. That baby grew up to live the most spectacular life of anyone who ever walked the planet. But He was met with such opposition that stakes were driven through His hands and feet on a wooden cross. A crown of thorns pierced His head, and a spear broke open His side producing a gushing river of blood and water. It was to forever serve as the autopsy of a broken heart.

His disciples stood near as He was placed in a borrowed tomb. They watched as the tomb was sealed.

They thought it was over.

They didn't know it was finished.

You see, it was those words, "It is finished!" that were whispered from the cross. They literally meant that the debt had been paid.

We each have sin in our lives. That sin separates us from God. We need a new start. His death gives us that.

We can invite Him to come into our lives and begin again.

You see, they knew He was dead but they didn't know that in three days, He would live again.

It is that life that He wants to pour into ours. The Bible tells us that He stands at the door and knocks. He wants to come into our lives to give us an about face, a new beginning. He is not a ghost. He is alive. You can begin that relationship with Him with a simple prayer. It can go something like this:

Dear Jesus, I know I am a sinner. I have done a lot of things wrong. I believe that You died on the cross to forgive me for my sins. I ask you to come into my life to be my Savior and Lord. Thank you for saving me.
Amen

We don't have to live under the ghosts of our past. Neither do we have to look for door knockers that speak scary words to bring us redemption. Our redemption was bought and paid for at the cross. The debt was paid.

Old Scrooge awoke to realize that he hadn't missed Christmas. You don't have to either!

Matthew 2

In Matthew 1:18-21 it says:

"This is how the birth of Jesus the Messiah came about: His mother Mary was pledged to be married to Joseph, but before they came together, she was found to be pregnant through the Holy Spirit. Because Joseph her husband was faithful to the law, and yet did not want to expose her to public disgrace, he had in mind to divorce her quietly.

But after he had considered this, an angel of the Lord appeared to him in a dream and said, 'Joseph Son of David, do not be afraid to take Mary home as your wife, because what is conceived in her is from the Holy Spirit. She will give birth to a son, and you are to give him the name Jesus, because He will save His people from their sins.'"

Day 33

I am reflecting this morning...thinking back to that moment in time when the phone rang and we were told that we had a two month old baby girl.

She owned nothing. She wore a little outfit but the agency had requested it back. When we went to pick her up, we didn't even have a blanket with us. We simply were not prepared for her arrival.

That seems odd to me today. We had been married for eight years and been on the adoption list for five. We had been through all of the interviews and home studies. But we weren't ready.

We had been told that all of the hearings to terminate parental rights were on a Tuesday. What they explained was that we would get the phone call to give us the good news that we were parents, but that we would not be able to meet our little one and bring her home until the next day. I knew that the twenty-four hours of holding my breath would not be possible unless I could fill the time. I would go then to pick-up everything we would need.

But that isn't how it happened. Even though she was expected, she came unexpectedly. When we got the call, we were told we could get her right away.

Suddenly our lives were changed.

We had expected her but she came unexpectedly.
The word spread quickly and all who heard it joined
with us in such joy. By that night all of our friends had
gone out shopping and poured gifts on our little girl.

We had everything we needed.

Matthew 2

The Magi, Wise Men, from the East had been expecting the arrival of the King. I am not quite sure how they knew to be watching, but they did. How long had it been? Had the word been passed down from the time of Daniel? Had they had opportunities to read what God had inspired? We are not told the answer to these questions but we know that they had been expecting this King. In Matthew 2:2 it tells us that they had seen HIS star in the east and they came to worship Him.

They had been expecting Him but He came unexpectedly. They weren't even quite sure where to find Him. They stopped for directions but they asked the wrong gas station attendant. His name was King Herod.

The Scripture records that he was *"disturbed"*. But he was not the only one. We are told that the news spread quickly and all of Jerusalem was disturbed. Israel had long since tired of holding their breath and waiting for their King. His arrival was disturbing.

Day 34

I believe that God has placed in women the need for beauty. We like to make things around us look nice, homey, charming, elegant, even if the base color is brown. Many men couldn't care less what color the pillows are that are on the couch or if the candy dish on the side table brings out the color of the threads in the tweed of the couch. We want the Christmas decorations on the mantle to coordinate with the Christmas tree. So when women decorate, it is, perhaps, part of the natural nesting process. Therefore, I know you will understand that when the brown wooden coffee table clashed with the new brown wood flooring, something significant had to be done.

Let me tell you first, that I have actually refinished furniture and most of it ended up being usable. Although I'm no expert, neither am I a complete novice. Therefore tackling the large, square, flea-market-find coffee table was not really a daunting task. I sanded it, took off the high gloss varnish finish (that I did not like) so I could give it a different look. Since most of my house is brown I decided to white wash it to give it a lighter brown appearance. This seemed easy enough...mix some white paint with some water, brush it into the wood, and then rub it down with a rag to give it that aged look I love. I HATED it.

Back to the sanding. I decided black was the way to go. This wouldn't be hard. I mixed black paint with water. I painted it on, brushed it into the wood and rubbed it in to give it that worn, kind of used look I love. I HATED it.

I added stain, English walnut, still not right. You see the problem was that the top of the table had wood grain going in two different directions. When I stained it or painted it, no matter how hard I tried, it was not taking the color correctly. I HATED it, back to the sanding.

Then I hit on a fantastic idea. I would find something to cover the top. I went to the craft store and bought some paper that looked like aged wood. I would just use a product to decopage it to the top and it would be done. Let me give you some advice...before you use a gluing product, make absolutely sure you like it. That stuff is really hard to get off. After three days of painting, sanding, gluing, staining, sanding, painting, staining, I realized that all of my choices didn't make it look better. They made it look worse. I was ready to throw up my hands, drag it to the curb with a sign that said, "Five dollars, I'll pay you for taking it off my hands."

I finally decided if this was ever going to be salvaged, there was only one way to go. I got out the paint stripper and started over. I worked to get off the layers. It wasn't easy and the coffee table bares the scars, but it's done.

It's now black and brown, a little white washed, with some paper still stuck in the corners of the top. It's a piece of furniture that the grandchildren can use as a coloring table and it won't hurt a thing. It is a reminder to me that my choices have consequences and they sometimes leave scars.

Matthew 2

Some choices we make, like my coffee table, have small consequences. Some choices we make have life altering consequences. But then there are choices that have eternal consequences. Herod made such a choice. We see in Matthew 2:2 that Magi came and asked Herod *"Where is the one who has been born king of the Jews. We saw his star when it rose and have come to worship him."* The Magi saw the star and they chose to come to worship. Herod's reaction was to be disturbed and called together the chief priests and teachers of the law. He asked them *"Where the Messiah was to be born?"*

"'In Bethlehem in Judea,' they replied" It was what the prophet had said in Micah 5:2. He called the Magi and found out exactly when the star had appeared. There was the testimony of the Magi, there was the witness of a real star, he had the word from the chief priests and teachers of the law, he had the word of the prophet, he had the Word of God. This was the love of God confronting him with the truth. God gave him so many chances. Herod even watched as the Magi left. You see both the Magi and Herod had choices to make.

The Magi went to Bethlehem with gifts.

Herod sent soldiers to Bethlehem with swords.

The Magi went to worship the Child.

Herod sent soldiers to kill the children.

The Magi met Jesus in Bethlehem.

Herod met Jesus at The Judgment.

Choices...

Day 35

Linda is one of the authors of this book and this is a story about her. It's not one that she would tell, but I think it's a story that needs to be told. So let me take you back to where this story begins.

Thanksgiving of 1974 our father was diagnosed with terminal cancer. It was eleven months later that he lost that battle, but as followers of Christ we never lose, we actually gain by stepping into eternity with Him. On September 16, 1975, we gathered to celebrate his life at the funeral. There is joy in knowing that someone is with the Lord, but there is also great sadness in saying good bye to a loved one.

We were all grieving but Linda read the enormous, overwhelming grief on our Mother's face. Linda breathed out a short little prayer. Many twenty-something young women would at this time in their lives be hoping and praying to meet their husband. And that is exactly where Linda was. She had been praying for the right man. But standing at the grave site her prayer was changed. "Lord, Mom needs me. She needs me for a while. So, Father, if You are going to bring someone into my life let me wait to meet him for at least two years."

A prayer for a gift of time.

And then not quite three weeks later, our grandmother (our mom's mother) passed away. I remember at her funeral standing at our Grandmother's grave and thinking that the dirt on Dad's grave had not even yet settled. In three short weeks our forty-nine year old mom had experienced a great deal of loss.

So Linda had gone to the Lord with this request. This may not have been a path that Linda would have originally chosen for herself but it was the journey that the Lord put her on. It became part of Linda's mission to bring our mother joy. Sometimes she would bring home infant sized ice cream cones, just a bite of something sweet, and it made Mother smile. Sometimes she brought home the giant, oversized, ice cream cones and they made Mother laugh. During an ice storm the electricity went off. They laughed hysterically wearing stocking caps and camping under quilts in the basement. They went out to eat together. Sometimes they would go to the mall on a whim. Both Mom and Linda loved snow and Linda's car was a tank. So even in the Ohio winter they would brave the snow storms just to go to browse the almost empty mall. They laughed together, they cried together and God brought healing.

God so graciously answered Linda's very unselfish request and she met the man she would marry on September 16, 1977. Isn't it miraculous how God answers sometimes so specifically because this was two years to the day that she had uttered that prayer?

It may have been to the exact hour. At Christmas time that year, the family got to meet him. He is a patient, kind, gentle giant and we knew instantly that he was a keeper.

Matthew 2

They saw it. It was there. Perhaps at first just a glimmer, but then as it grew brighter, they knew; it was a brand new shining star. Nothing like this had ever before happened in the night sky. This wasn't just any star. This star pointed to a promise about to be fulfilled.

They were called Magi, astrologers, star gazers, some of royal birth, the wisest men in the realm. They were the ones used to interpret dreams and read the secrets in the stars. But this new star couldn't just be read; this star had to be followed.

The Bible doesn't tell us exactly where these wise-men came from. It says the east. A likely guess is Babylon. A trip from Babylon to Bethlehem would not have been easy. Thieves, robbers, treacherous terrain would have made it a difficult journey. This would not have been a path they would perhaps have chosen for themselves, but it was the path that God put them on. The Bible doesn't tell us how they knew to come seeking the King of the Jews. Daniel had lived as a wise-man in Babylon. Perhaps it was his legacy of faith in God and in His Word. The scripture does tell us in Numbers 24:17: *"I see him, but not now; I behold him, but not near. A star will come out of Jacob; a scepter will rise out of Israel."*

Maybe it was this Scripture that guided them. Matthew 2 only records that they came and asked, *"Where is the one who has been born King of the Jews?"* They saw His star in the east and they came for one reason...to worship this King.

Day 36

My husband just came back from a conference. He brought me a gift. Now isn't that sweet? It means that he was thinking about me.

Well, yes, but I want to share with you a little about his gift giving history.

One day he came into my classroom, wearing his best black suit and laid a rose on the desk of my assistant and an equally beautiful rose on mine. He was only there for a moment.

My assistant was delighted. She said, "Kris, that was so nice!"

I looked at her and smiled. "Don't get too excited. I think he just came from a funeral."

I was right.

Flowers from dead people's caskets are not all that sweet even if it is frugal. You see my husband is a pastor and sometimes a few flowers are left behind. Because he doesn't want the people to witness the flowers just being discarded, he takes them to hand to the family. If he ends up with a flower or two left in his hand he brings them to me.

The gift from the conference was equally as lovely. It was a small blood red colored sponge brain. Yes, you read this correctly. It was a brain.

It is actually the second time he has brought home a brain. I don't think he thought it helped the last time. Now that I think about it, both times he was at the conference with the "I have a big brain and you have a tiny brain" nephew. Maybe he was influenced by him.

I do know that the brain was free.

Roses from the dead and free brains from a conference don't always add up to the best way to express love.

There are not a lot of ways to spin that to make "I was just thinking about you" sound precious.

Just a little advice to any guys reading this, stay away from those gifts for the ladies you love.

I will say this, people see gifts from all different angles. (Do you remember the lederhosen episode?) But the gift giving tradition at Christmas has at its core a beauty that is impossible to express. Wise men from the East had gifts in their hands that hinted at the worship in their hearts. I think they knew that the gifts they would lay at His feet could never be compared to the gift they would receive.

He was the Gift.

John 3:16 says it like this: *"For God so loved the world that he gave his one and only Son, that whoever believes in Him shall not perish but have eternal life."*

They went home with changed lives. There is no better gift than that.

Matthew 2

Have you ever been to a baby shower? Plush toys, a delicately crocheted blanket, tiny shoes, even tinier booties, frilly dresses, soft pastel sleepers, almost collectively everyone takes a deep breath followed by "oohs" and "aahs" and "isn't that cute" or "I love that, it's just so sweet"

But let's step back and examine Matthew 2:11. The gifts that were showered on the baby Jesus were gold, frankincense, and myrrh. The Magi traveled quite a distance for this shower. They came from the East carrying their gifts. But why these gifts? Why gold, frankincense and myrrh? Gold is useful, it would have been a monetary exchange. When Joseph and Mary had to flee with Jesus to Egypt this would have supported them. But gold hints at something beyond its usefulness. Gold is the gift of kings. It is for palaces and royalty. Frankincense was a fragrant spice, part of the incense used in the temple by the priests. Frankincense speaks of the priesthood. But then there is myrrh, and this is not a gift that one would normally bring to a baby. This aromatic resin was used in preparing a body for burial.

So do you see the significance?

Day 37

Three bathrooms, six grown children, six spouses, and a whole bunch of little ones, all visiting mom for Christmas, and...the flu. Not the quiet, headache, sleeping kind of flu, but rather the "I NEED TO USE THE BATHROOM NOW!" kind of flu. Everyone and I mean everyone except my one sister and I and our four month old babies, got the flu.

People met each other on the steps coming and going from the bathrooms to the bed. It wasn't pretty. It wasn't Christmas at its best. It wasn't chestnuts roasting and pies baking, and the sweet scent of pine in the air. It was more Pine-Sol than pine, more grave than gravy. The sounds emanating from the house were not carols or lilting melodies. The laundry crawled from the laundry room. Toilet paper was a treasured commodity. Chicken soup was the order of the day.

Our younger brother had just returned from his honeymoon with his new wife. They had met at college and we didn't yet know her well. Yep. They got sick too, in fact, we're pretty sure they were the ones who introduced this ebola virus to Mom's. Funny thing about a common enemy, it bonds you. Our new sister-in-law became one of us, not an in-law, but rather a sister. Who would have thought that there could be a gift behind the flu?

Matthew 2

Have you noticed that when confronted with greatness, we humans react? At sports events during
an incredible play people respond with yells and
screams and cheers. When someone famous walks
into a room, the crowd stands to their feet. When
beautiful inspiring music is played, the audience
erupts with outbursts of applause. Why? Because
it is in us, we were made to express our awe and
amazement. When the wise-men saw Jesus, they
were overjoyed. They were overcome with a desire to
express their exuberant gladness.

But, they didn't rise to their feet; they knelt at His.
They didn't yell and scream; they worshiped.

They came looking for the King of the Jews; they met
the King of Kings.

They presented their gifts; they received a greater gift.

The Bible says God warned them to return home
by a different route because Herod did not want to
worship Jesus, he wanted to kill Him. So the magi
obeyed God and went home a different way. What is
interesting is that the phrase, "a different route", can
also mean a different manner of life. In other words,
they went home different. They were changed men.
They had worshiped at the feet of Immanuel, God
with us, and they would never be the same again.

When we respond to the greatness of men, it is exciting, exhilarating. But when we respond to the greatness of God, we are changed. True worship changes us. We go home in a different manner of life.

Day 38

As I have said before, gifts were not very common at our home. So when Dad came home one beautiful autumn day and called us outside, telling us he had a surprise, we were thrilled. This happened... well, it almost never happened. We stood with great anticipation while he reached into the old olive-drab Volkswagen bus that was just about the only vehicle on the planet big enough to transport eight people. He pulled out five brand new red...RAKES, one for each of us to have for our very own. We lived on a three acre wooded lot.

But for Christmas there were wonderful things. As a young girl, one of the gifts I wanted most was a doll. Over the years, I had quite a few. The one I remember best was a life size baby doll. She came with clothes and real baby care things. I was thrilled. Yes, she was beautiful, but she was not perfect. I carried her to my grandmother's house for Christmas dinner and treated her just like she was a tiny person. But there must have been a flaw in the plastic because by the time I got home late that Christmas night she had a chip out of her left hand. By the next evening her entire hand had broken off. My parents should have probably taken her back to the store, but returning toys was not really on their radar screen. But even if they had wanted to I'm not sure I could have parted with her.

You see, she was mine. Not only that, she was hurt and in my child's mind, she needed protection. I do remember looking at my sisters' dolls and wondering why mine was broken and theirs were not but it didn't change the fact that I already loved her. I probably took better care of her because she was broken. Maybe better care than I would have after the "new" had worn off and she became just another one of the toys left in the black hole we called our play room. Some years later I carried her lovingly to an orphanage hoping someone would not see her as a broken toy, but rather as a wounded child and love her like I had.

As an adult I look back on that and I wonder if when we are broken or wounded, God holds us closer to His heart so we can be protected during those trying times. Oh it's easy to look at someone else and wonder why they are not going through the trial, but maybe, just maybe, God is holding us close during that time and that is indeed a gift.

Genesis 3

Perfection: it began. Two humans created perfectly by God, no sin, no sorrow, no sadness, no sickness, no separation. It was just perfection, purity, sweet fellowship, exquisite beauty, and then a choice. The garden was perfect. Every tree from which they could possibly want to eat was available except for one. God said that they were not to eat from the tree of the knowledge of good and evil.

And then the serpent's wicked voice broke through the perfection and asked, *"Did God really say that you could not eat from any tree in the garden?"*

Eve listened. She looked. She touched. She tasted. She gave some to Adam and he also ate. Then suddenly...

Brokenness: it began. These two humans were separated from God. Disobedience, disease, destruction, despair, discord, and death entered the world. This was the price for one single sin.

But in the midst of that our loving Heavenly Father looked at the brokenness and breathed out the promise of the Christmas story. The seed of the woman would crush the head of the serpent. Genesis 3:15.

Day 39

It's time for a new year, so let's close up the last one. Let's take all of last year's sorrows, broken promises, failed resolutions, missed opportunities, mangled schedules and stuff them down deep inside of a very large box, close the lid, lock it up and throw away the key. Let's drag it out to the curb with all of the torn Christmas wrappings, empty gift bags, and thrown out junk that's going to be picked up in next week's trash. This is, after all, a new year, a time for new beginnings and a new resolve. Let's get rid of the old.

Or wait a minute, do we really want to do that? If we throw out all the pain, the sorrow, the broken promises, what might we miss?

Could there possibly be a gift even in some of those moments of difficulty?

Was there something we experienced through that sorrow that brought us closer to the Lord? Maybe that is worth remembering.

Was there a trust that grew in God's promises even though some of men's promises were broken? Can we hang onto that trust?

Is there a way that the failings of last year can help us achieve success this year, because we learned to place our plans in God's hands?

Did we miss an opportunity over the last twelve months? If so could that make us more aware this year to not overlook a chance to further the kingdom of God?

Did our schedules own us, and if so could we turn them over to the Lord and let Him direct our steps? In other words, what did God teach us last year through the stuff that we lived through?

On this day of new beginnings as we start a new day, a new month, a new year, what did we learn that can help us walk closer to the Lord during this New Year?

John 1

Adam and Eve sinned. They absolutely blew it, but
so did I, today and last week and last month and last
year. I blew it so badly that a part of me wants to
never again look back. Maybe Adam and Eve felt like
that as well. So did they ever look back? The Bible
doesn't tell us but it seems logical that they did. Was
there sadness? I am sure there was as Adam toiled
in the ground and the sweat dripped from his brow.
Was there regret? It's hard to imagine that there
wasn't, as he had to pull the weeds and thorns that
had grown up among the crops. Was there loneliness
and grief? They were separated from God so the
pain that Eve experienced as she gave birth to her
children may have been even more magnified.

But they had something that they could always look
forward to. That was God's Word. He had promised
that One would come. We've looked at both Luke
and Matthew. Another of the Gospels expounds a
little more on the Christmas story because it takes us
back to the beginning. In John 1:1 it says *"In the beginning was the Word, and the Word was with God,
and the Word was God"*. Verse 14 continues, *"The
Word became flesh and made His dwelling among
us."* Jesus, the Word of God, came. In the garden
Adam and Eve lost everything because of one sin.

In another garden Jesus began the work that would buy it all back. Adam worked by the sweat of his brow. From Jesus' brow, He sweat drops of blood. Adam dealt with thorns. Jesus wore them as a crown. Pain entered the world. Jesus experienced so much pain that a new word, 'excruciating', had to be invented. The word literally means 'of the cross'. Adam and Eve ate from a tree that brought them death. Jesus died on a tree that brought us life. Adam and Eve committed one sin. Jesus committed no sin but took on ALL sin. Adam and Eve had to leave paradise.

Jesus opens the door for us to enter Heaven. Now how about that for Christmas gifts and new beginnings!

Day 40

The Christmas trees are coming down, the decorations put away, the merchandise in the stores is nearly gone. Not so many houses twinkle with lights and the Christmas carols aren't being played. We're saying goodbye to Christmas. But Christmas isn't something we can put away in a box, and we never really say goodbye. The Christmas story continues.

It began with the visit of angels and ended with the visit of kings. We are told of a baby wrapped in strips of cloth and lovingly laid in a wooden manger. But very soon that child would become a Man. He would be stripped of His clothing, harshly beaten, laid on a wooden cross, and firmly nailed there. Mary's eyes that dripped with tears of joy at His birth would drip with tears of grief and sorrow at His death. The night skies that were lit bright with Heaven's Glory at His birth would give way to day skies that turned dark as night at His death.

The Christmas story: a birth...a death...and then a resurrection. Oh no, Christmas isn't over, because Easter is on its way.

Luke 24:5-6

"...Why do you look for the living among the dead, He is not here: he has risen."

HE HAS RISEN!

Take a deep breath...it's Easter!

Learn More

Learn more, explore additional writings,
and contact K.L. Kandel at **www.klkandel.com**.